CLASSIC SERMONS
ON
OLD TESTAMENT
PROPHETS

The Kregel Classic Sermons Series

KREGEL CLASSIC   SERMONS SERIES

CLASSIC SERMONS ON OLD TESTAMENT PROPHETS

Compiled by
Warren W. Wiersbe

kregel
PUBLICATIONS

Grand Rapids, MI 49501

Classic Sermons on Old Testament Prophets
Compiled by Warren W. Wiersbe

Published by Kregel Publications, a division of Kregel, Inc., P.O. Box 2607, Grand Rapids, MI 49501. Kregel Publications provides trusted, biblical publications for Christian growth and service. Your comments and suggestions are valued.

For more information about Kregel Publications, visit our web site at: www.kregel.com

Cover photo: © PhotoDisc

ISBN 0-8254-4084-x

Printed in the United States of America
1 2 3 4 5 / 04 03 02 01 00

Contents

List of Scripture Texts

Preface

THE *Kregel Classic Sermons Series* is an attempt to assemble and publish meaningful sermons from master preachers about significant themes. These are *sermons,* not essays or chapters taken from books about themes. Not all of these sermons could be called great, but all of them are *meaningful.* They apply the truths of the Bible to the needs of the human heart, which is something that all effective preaching must do.

While some are better known than others, all of the preachers whose sermons I have selected had important ministries and were highly respected in their day. The fact that a sermon is included in this volume does not mean that either the compiler or the publisher agrees with or endorses everything that the man did, preached, or wrote. The sermon is here because it has a valuable contribution to make.

These are sermons about *significant* themes. The pulpit is no place to play with trivia. The preacher has thirty minutes in which to help mend broken hearts, change defeated lives, and save lost souls; he can never accomplish this demanding ministry by distributing homiletical tidbits. In these difficult days we do not need clever pulpiteers who discuss the times; we need dedicated ambassadors who will preach the eternities.

The reading of these sermons can enrich your spiritual life. The studying of them can enrich your skills as an interpreter and expounder of God's truth. However God uses these sermons in your life and ministry, my prayer is that His church around the world will be encouraged and strengthened by them.

WARREN W. WIERSBE

Habakkuk: On His Watchtower

Alexander Whyte (1836–1921) was known as "the last of the Puritans," and certainly his sermons were surgical as he magnified the glory of God and exposed the sinfulness of sin. He succeeded the noted Robert S. Candlish as pastor of Free Saint George's and reigned from that influential Edinburgh pulpit for nearly forty years. He loved to "dig again in the old wells" and share with his people truths learned from the devotional masters of the past. His evening Bible courses attracted the young people and led many into a deeper walk with God.

This sermon was taken from Whyte's book *Lord, Teach Us to Pray,* published by Hodder and Stoughton.

ALEXANDER WHYTE

1

Habakkuk: On His Watchtower

Lord, teach us to pray. (Luke 11:1)

I will stand upon my watch, and set me upon the tower.
(Habakkuk 2:1)

HABAKKUK'S TOWER was not built of stone and lime. Hiram's
Tyrian workmen, with all their skill in hewn stone, timber, iron,
and brass, had no hand in building Habakkuk's tower. "The
name of the Lord" was Habakkuk's high tower. The truth and
the faithfulness and the power of God—these things were the
deep and broad foundations of Habakkuk's high tower, into
which he continually escaped, and from the high top of which
he was wont to look out upon the land and up to his God. God's
grace and mercy and long-suffering were the doors and stairs,
were the walls and battlements of Habakkuk's high tower. God's
sure salvation was the golden and the far-shining roof of it. "Art
thou not from everlasting," prayed this prophet as often as he
again stood upon his watch and set himself upon his tower—
"O LORD my God, mine Holy One? we shall not die" (Hab. 1:12).

The Chaldeans had, by this time, overrun the whole land.
Judah and Jerusalem had for long been full of all but unpardon-
able sin. God's chosen and covenant people had despised and

9

forsaken God. The law of God was "slacked" until the land was
full of all unrighteousness. And thus it was that this judgment
of God had already gone forth against Judah and Jerusalem:
"Lo, I raise up the Chaldeans, that bitter and hasty nation, which
shall march through the breadth of the land, to possess the
dwellingplaces that are not their's. They are terrible and dreadful. . . . Their horses also are swifter than the leopards, and are
more fierce than the evening wolves . . . they shall fly as the eagle
that hasteth to eat. They shall come all for violence . . . and they
shall gather the captivity as the sand" (vv. 6–9). And it was so. It
was very much as if the Turks of our day had been let loose on
England, Scotland, and Edinburgh.

It was amid the indescribable cruelties and horrors of the
invasion and possession of Judah and Jerusalem by the
Chaldeans that Habakkuk took up his burden. And Habakkuk
the prophet was alone. He was alone and had no fellow in the
midst of all those desolate years. Alone!—and with his faith very
hard pressed between God, in His righteous anger on the one
hand, and guilty Judah, under her great agony and oppression
on the other hand.

And we have this great and noble-hearted prophet in all the
heat and burden of his work—in his faith, his prayer, and his
songs—all set before us with extraordinary beauty and impres-
siveness in this wonderful little book. A book little in size, indeed, but a book rich and great in divine substance, and in
intellectual and spiritual power of every kind. "O LORD, how long
shall I cry, and thou wilt not hear! even cry out unto thee of
violence, and thou wilt not save! Why dost thou shew me iniquity, and cause me to behold grievance? for spoiling and violence are before me . . . the wicked doth compass about the
righteous. . . . I will stand upon my watch, and I set me upon
the tower, and will watch to see what he will say unto me. . . .
And the LORD answered me, and said, Write the vision, and make
it plain upon tables, that he may run that readeth it" (1:2–2:2).
And, at that, the prophet immediately came down from his tower
and had great tablets made by the workman. He wrote this text

upon the tables—this text, "The just shall live by his faith" (2:4). And he had the tables hung upon the temple walls, and on the gates and on the marketplaces of the city until he who ran from the oppression of the enemy, as well as he who ran to take up arms against the oppressor, might read the legend—this legend—that "the just shall live by his faith" (Rom. 1:17; Gal. 3:11; Heb. 10:38). The Chaldeans understood not the tables, but the oppressed people of God understood them—until it abides a proverb, and an encouragement, and a doctrine, and a sure hope to this day that "the just shall live by faith."

In a profound and far-reaching passage—in two profound and far-reaching passages indeed—Pascal impresses on us, out of such Scripture as this, that our own passions are our only enemies. Our real enemies, with all their cruelty and all their oppression, come up upon us, not out of Chaldea, but out of our own hearts. Chaldea, with all her cruel and aggrandizing ambition, would never have been allowed to cross the Jordan and let loose in Judah but for Judah's sin. And it was Judah's continuing transgression and persisting impenitence that kept the Chaldeans in possession of Judah and Jerusalem. All which is written in the prophet, with Pascal's profound and spiritual interpretation of the prophet, for our learning, and for our very closest and most practical application to ourselves. Let this, then, be laid to heart by all God's people, that their sinful hearts and sinful lives, while they are in this present life, are always, more or less, like the land of Judah under the cruel occupation of the Chaldeans.

Our sins, my brethren, have brought the bitterest of all our chastisements upon us, that is, upon our souls. Not every child of God among us has yet spirituality of mind enough, or personal experience enough, to see and to admit that. Judah did not easily and willingly see and admit that. But Habakkuk in his day, and Pascal in our day, saw it. They both saw it and wrote powerfully and convincingly and with splendid comfort concerning it. And many of God's people among yourselves, by much experience, by much prayer, by a sinful heart and a holy life taken together, are themselves prophets—prophets and philosophers, wise men, that is—in the deepest things, both of God and of the soul of man.

And one of those deepest things is just this—that *God chastises sin by means of sin*. He employs the remaining sinfulness of the sanctified heart as His last and His best instrument for reaching down into the depths of the heart to bring about its complete discovery, complete correction, and complete purification. There is no tyranny so terrible, there is no invasion and captivity of the soul one-thousandth part so horrible and so hated of all God's saints, as is their captivity to their own sins. Those whose true torments and tortures come, never from without, but always from within. Those whose abidingly bad hearts are being made God's cruellest scourge—both for their past sins and for their present sinfulness—*they* will consent and subscribe to all that this great prophet says in the terrible account that he gives of the Chaldeans. "That bitter and hasty nation, which shall march through the breadth of the land, to possess the dwellingplaces that are not their's. They are terrible and dreadful" (Hab. 1:6–7). "He is a proud man . . . who enlargeth his desire as hell, and is as death, and cannot be satisfied. . . . Shall they not rise up suddenly that shall bite thee, and awake that shall vex thee, and thou shalt be for booties unto them?" (2:5, 7). All of which is but a cruel parable to some of us concerning our own sins.

So truly does our God also, in His grace and truth, still make His own so sovereign and so spiritual use of our remaining and deep-rooted sinfulness. In His wisdom and in His love, at one stroke, He does these two most divine things: securing the greatest depth, the greatest inwardness, and the greatest spirituality for our sanctification; and, at the same time, securing, more and more every day, our fear and hatred and horror at our own hearts, as at nothing else on earth or in hell. Is that your mind, my brethren? Is that your experience? "The spiritual understood Chaldea of their passions," says Pascal. "The unspiritual and the still carnal-minded understood it of Chaldea only. The term *enemy*," he adds, "and Chaldea is obscure and ambiguous only to the unspiritual in mind and in heart." Let all students of Holy Scripture, and of the heart of man, study Pascal.

Look, now, at that man of God who is like Habakkuk in our own days. Look at that prophet upon his tower in our own city. He has climbed up far above us, his fellows, into a calm and clear air. He has so climbed by means of much prayer, much meditation, and much secret self-denial of many kinds. He has a time and a place of retreat, of purification, and of exaltation of the mind that we know nothing of. He may be a minister—most likely he is—or he may be a busy business man, as sometimes he is. He may be well known to us to be a man like Habakkuk; or, he may be hidden even from himself. Sometimes he is old, and, not seldom, he is young. In any case, he is our Habakkuk. Habakkuk, with his own burden and sometimes with ours. "O LORD," he cries on his watch, "how long shall I cry, and thou wilt not hear!" (1:2). "I will stand upon my watch, and set me upon the tower, and will watch to see what he will say unto me" (2:1).

There are men among us who do not neglect prayer, who yet sadly neglect to watch and wait for God's promised answer to their prayers. Prayer, when we think of it and perform it aright, is a magnificent—and venturesome—thing for any man to do. For prayer builds and fits out and mans and launches a frail vessel of faith on the deep and wide sea of God's sovereignty, and sets her sails for a harbor nothing short of heaven. And, then, the wise merchantman gives God and his ship time to be on her way back again. Then, like Habakkuk, he sets himself on his high tower. All his interests are now up there. As Paul has it, all his conversation is in heaven. All his treasures and all his affections are launched on that sea-adventure he is now so intensely watching up there.

I am convinced, my brethren, that we lose many answers to our prayers—not so much because we do not pray, as because we do not go up to our tower to watch for and to welcome

God's answers to our prayers. "Why should I answer?" our God may well say to His waiting and ministering angels. "Why should I answer him? He pays no attention to My answer to his prayer. He is never on his watch when I send My answer. And, even when I do send My answers to his house and to his heart, he takes them and holds them as common and everyday things. He never wonders at My grace to him. He never performs his vow for My goodness to him. He holds a thousand—he and his— of My benefits, but he does not seem to know it." My brethren, I am as sure as I am standing here, that we would all get far more, and far more wonderful answers to prayer, if only we were far more on the outlook for them. Habakkuk never made a holier or a more fruitful resolve than when he said, "I will stand upon my watch, and set me upon the tower, and will watch to see what he will say unto me."

There were many shapes and sizes of towers in the land of Judah, and they were put, by the people of Judah and Jerusalem, to many and various uses. Their city walls would rise up, all around their cities, into strong towers both for defense and for beauty. Immense towers were built also by the military engineers of those days on frontiers, on passes, on peaks, and on exposed situations. To protect a great well also, a strong stone tower would be built to secure safety to the flocks of cattle and sheep that came to the well and to its waters to drink. No vineyard worth anything to its owner was ever left without its tower—both to lodge the keeper of the vineyard and to be the home of the grape-gatherers at the grape-gathering season. Until, all over the land, and all around the city, all kinds of towers stood up to give life, strength, and beauty to the whole landscape.

And so it is in the church of Christ. Until He who sees His own holy land as no eye but His sees it—He who sees every soldier and watchman, every vinedresser, and every keeper of sheep in it; He who has His sleepless eye on every praying and expecting soul—He sees His Holy Land and His Holy City encompassed, ramparted, and ornamented with ten thousand such towers. And He never long leaves any such tower without its proper and appointed vision. For, as often as any watching soul says, "I will stand upon my watch, and will set me upon my tower," the Lord who spoke to Habakkuk says to us the same thing: "Though it tarry, wait for it; because it will surely come, it will not tarry" (2:3). And, there is nothing that our Lord says so often as just *this*—He says it every morning, indeed, and every night to all who wait for Him—*"The just,"* He says without ceasing, *"shall live by his faith."* Until one tower answers that vision, that password and watchword, to another; until all the land rings with it and echoes with it. The Lord speaks it first to Habakkuk, and Habakkuk to Paul, and Paul to Rome and Galatia, and Rome and Galatia to us.

Still the same counsel and comfort keeps on counseling all the dwellers in their lonely towers, "The just shall live by faith." What Habakkuk wrote six hundred years before Christ on the gates and walls and pillars of Jerusalem—that very same word of God—the Holy Spirit of God is writing on the tables that are in the believing hearts of all God's people still: "Being justified by faith, we have peace with God" (Rom. 5:1). "By grace are ye saved through faith" (Eph. 2:8). "The just shall live by his faith." He shall live—not so much by the fulfillment of all God's promises, nor by God's full answers to his prayers and expectations, nor by the full deliverance of his soul from his bitter enemies, nor by the full and final expulsion of the Chaldeans—but he shall live, amid all these troubles and until they come to an end forever—by his firm faith in God and in the future that is all in God's hand. And thus it is that whatever our oppression and persecution may be, whatever our prayer and wherever and whatever our waiting tower, still this old and ever new vision and answer comes: faith, faith, and faith only. Rest and trust in God. Commit your way to God. Be your enemy from beyond the Euphrates, or be he out of the evil of your own heart, keep on in prayer. Keep on watching. Keep yourself on your Tower. Keep saying, keep singing:

> For thou art God that dost
> To me salvation send,
> And I upon Thee all the day
> Expecting do attend.

Go up every new day into Habakkuk's high tower and take up his prayer and his hope. Are You not from everlasting, O Lord, my God, mine Holy One? I shall not die. Say *you* also, "I shall not die." *That* is faith. *That* is the very faith by which the just have been enabled to live in all ages of the church of God. No man ever died under the hand of his enemy who so believed in God, and in the power and grace of God. You may sometimes be afraid that you are to be left to die in your sin and sorrow. So was Habakkuk sometimes. "O LORD, I have heard thy speech, and was afraid" (Hab. 3:2). Habakkuk was afraid to face the whole long, unbroken, unrelieved life of faith, and of *faith only*. Habakkuk would be up on his tower again to see if there were no signs of the Chaldeans leaving the land. At another time, he would stand upon his tower and look if none of Judah's old alliances were coming to her help. But still the full vision of his salvation tarried until he came to seek his salvation, not in any outward thing whatsoever; not even in complete deliverance from the Chaldeans, but in God—whether the Chaldeans were in possession of Judah and Jerusalem, or driven out of it. Until, taught of God, as he dwelt more and more with God in his high tower, Habakkuk was able to rise and attain to this—to this which is one of the highest attainments of faith and hope and love in all the Old Testament: "Yet I will rejoice in the LORD, I will joy in the God of my salvation. The LORD God is my strength, and he will make my feet like hinds' feet, and he will make me to walk upon mine high places" (vv. 18–19).

The Chaldeans with all their overwhelming invasions and with all their cruel oppressions have, then, been made Habakkuk's salvation. They took possession of dwelling places that were not theirs, until Habakkuk was compelled to seek a dwelling place that even they, with all their horses like leopards and all their horsemen like evening wolves, could not invade. They had hunted Habakkuk all his life up into his high tower until he is now far more of his time in his high tower than he is on the street or even in the temple of Jerusalem. And until, at last, Habakkuk has come to *this,* that he asks for no more in this world but to be able to *walk* on his "high place" into which he has been accustomed so often to climb. In Paul's seraphic words, Habakkuk's whole conversation is now in heaven. He has gone up upon his high tower so often and has set himself for such long seasons on his watch that he is now far more in heaven than on earth. Habakkuk will not only, all his remaining days, "watch" and "wait" on his high tower, but Habakkuk will *walk* there. He will *dwell* there. His true home and his sure dwelling place will be up *there.* Until, when the "beatific vision" comes—which will soon come to Habakkuk and will not tarry—it will find him walking, and waiting for it on his high places. "If ye then be risen with Christ, seek those things which are above, where Christ sitteth on the right hand of God. Set your affection on things above, not on things on the earth. . . . When Christ, who is our life, shall appear, then shall ye also appear with him in glory" (Col. 3:1–4).

Daniel: A Man of Excellent Spirit

George Campbell Morgan (1863–1945) was the son of a British Baptist preacher and preached his first sermon when he was thirteen years old. He had no formal training for the ministry, but his tireless devotion to the study of the Bible helped him to become one of the leading Bible teachers of his day. Rejected by the Methodists, he was ordained into the Congregational ministry. He was associated with Dwight L. Moody in the Northfield Bible conferences and was an itinerant Bible teacher. He is best known as the pastor of the Westminster Chapel, London (1904–1917 and 1933–1943). During his second term there, he had Dr. D. Martyn Lloyd-Jones as his associate.

He published more than sixty books and booklets, and his sermons are found in *The Westminster Pulpit* (London: Hodder and Stoughton, 1906–1916). This sermon was taken from volume 8.

2

Daniel: A Man of Excellent Spirit

Then this Daniel was distinguished above the presidents and
satraps, because an excellent spirit was in him; and the king
thought to set him over the whole realm. (Daniel 6:3 ASV)

THE STORY OF Daniel is very old and fascinating. All who had the
advantage of godly training and that supremest advantage in the
life of a child of a mother who told Bible stories in the early
days remember how they loved the story of Daniel. I believe that
as I read it for our lesson, in the heart of every hearer there
came again the consciousness of the old fascination and the old
interest. The story of Daniel is fascinating because it reveals the
possibilities of godliness in the midst of the circumstances of
ungodliness. Daniel and his friends in that age long ago were
loyal to God even in the land of their captors and amid all the
enticements of the court. In such circumstances perhaps the
subtlest of all temptations assail the man of faith. It is so much
easier to float with the stream than to stem it. The principle of
accommodation appeals so strongly to that lurking desire for
ease, which is one of the sure evidences of the fall of the human
race, that it needs very definite courage to resist, to be godly
amid ungodliness, to take a definite and positive stand for
principle where everything seems to be against principle.

The key to Daniel's splendid fidelity may be found in the statement of my text, repeated in other parts of the book: "an excellent spirit was in him." This statement literally means that in Daniel spirit predominated, was uppermost, was enthroned. We are accustomed to use the word *excellent* with other values and intentions, all of which may be right in certain connections. For instance, we say that *excellent* means fine, noble, admirable, and we are justified in thus defining it. But the etymology of the word has another signification. Excellent is something that excels, goes beyond, predominates, and the word translated "excellent" in our text carries exactly that meaning. We may with perfect accuracy read our text thus—it would not be rhythmic or admirable as a translation, but at least it would be accurate—"A spirit that excelled was in him," a spirit that projected was in him. Not flesh, but spirit was the chief thing.

This truth is evident at the very beginning of the story of Daniel. To him, it was not the king's dainties or wine from the king's table that were the principal things, but rectitude, which means life harmonizing with the infinite, the true, the eternal. The principal thing in Daniel was not the physical, though he was fair, ruddy, and splendid. Spirit was the dominant factor in the personality of this man. Daniel was not a man who thought of himself within the physical as possessing a spirit; he thought of himself within the spiritual as possessing a body. "An excellent spirit was in him." He was a man who began life in the spiritual and from that center governed the material. He was not a man who began life in the material, and from that circumference crushed and bruised and killed the spiritual. In other words, Daniel was a man proportioned after the pattern and ideal of God. In himself, and in all his relationships, he recognized that the supreme quantity, the supreme quality, was spirit. He was "a man of an excellent spirit."

Let us, then, examine the qualities of spirit manifested in the life story of the man in whom spirit excelled and was the principal thing. I want to say four things about Daniel as revealing what life is, where spirit excels, where it is dominant, and where it is enthroned. This man of excellent spirit, in whom spirit excels, was, first, a man of purpose; second, a man of prayers; third, a man of perception; and, finally, a man of power. The first two things tell the cause; the second two describe the effect. The cause, or inspiration, of all this man's life story is found in the fact that he was a man of purpose and a man of prayer, and the effect is seen in the fact that he was a man of perception and a man of power. *Purpose* and *prayer*, these are the words that indicate our responsibility. *Perception* and *power*, these are the words that indicate what will follow in some way in the life of every man in whom spirit is dominant and who, therefore, is a man of purpose and a man of prayer.

Daniel Was a Man of Purpose

"Daniel purposed in his heart that he would not defile himself with the king's dainties" (Dan. 1:8). Notice carefully what this means. Purpose is at the beginning of every thing. Directly after finding himself in a place of peril he "purposed in his heart." This is the matter of supreme importance. Thousands of men drift into evil courses for lack of a definite and positive committal of themselves to some position, for lack of having purpose, something settled in their hearts. To delay in the moment of the first consciousness of perilous surroundings is to compromise presently, and, unless we are very careful, it is finally to apostatize. Daniel speaks to us today in no uncertain tone, and the message he utters at the very beginning is:

> Dare to be a Daniel,
>   Dare to stand alone,
>   Dare to have a purpose firm,
>   Dare to make it known!

That may be doggerel, but it is philosophy—the deepest secret of life for every young man or woman. I would to God that I could impress that thought on all young people! Purpose in a man's life is all-important. It affords him anchorage in the time of storm, creates for him a base in the day of battle. To have committed oneself to some definite thing is always of value in every walk of life. When a man has formed his purpose, he is halfway to victory. That is so with a boy who is looking forward to his life's work. When he knows what his purpose is, he is halfway to victory. He is not all the way to victory. It is quite possible to have formed that purpose, yet never to reach the goal; but it is equally certain that the goal cannot be reached without purpose.

The first thing for a man to do is to define the inner and deepest thing in his life. Underlying his life somewhere, every man has a purpose in the divine economy. Daniel found it, named it, announced it, and stood by it. It is quite impossible for a man to live without a purpose of some sort. Purpose lies at the back of will, and purpose operates through all activity. Some men have a score of purposes, but never one named, defined, or announced to which they are committed. In matters political, social, in all departments of human life, it is the man who has some definite purpose who is likely to arrive somewhere. I am sorely tempted to use an Americanism. I will. It is the man who has a purpose who *gets there!* As in the smaller, weaker, lower things of life, it is true that a man needs a purpose definite and announced; so also it is true supremely in matters of the spirit, in things of Christian life and service.

Daniel's purpose was a very simple one and yet sublime—simple in its expression, sublime in its great underlying principle. What was the simple purpose announced as he came down into the midst of the Chaldean court and its corruption? I will not touch the king's dainties; I will not drink the king's wine! That is the simplicity of the purpose but not the sublimity of it. What was the underlying reason? "[He] purposed in his heart that he would not defile himself with the king's dainties, nor with the wine which he drank" (Dan. 1:8). He purposed in his heart that his spirit was the supreme thing. He would not permit fleshly indulgence of any sort to rub the bloom from spiritual life, to weaken the nerve of spiritual endeavor, to dim the vision of spiritual outlook. He purposed that he would not defile *himself*. He was a man of excellent spirit, offspring of God, kin of the eternal, child and heir of the infinite, and he said, "My purpose is not to defile myself." Purpose found expression in his case in refusing the things that were likely to weaken the tabernacle of his flesh, and so defile the indwelling spirit which was himself. Daniel's deepest purpose was loyalty to God expressed in separation from the corrupting influences of his position. Because he stood there at the beginning, he was strong and victorious through all the coming days.

My brothers, I urge on you the importance of having a purpose and declaring it, of committing yourselves absolutely and positively, not merely in the sanctuary, but everywhere and always to some clearly defined position. Today, amid the allurements and enticements of a godless age, let every man purpose in his heart that he will be loyal to Jesus Christ. That is the sufficient purpose for all life today. You and I live in a much easier age than Daniel lived in, with forces at our disposal far more potent than had Daniel. This age may be more complex in its temptations, more subtle and insidious in the way it is likely to spoil men, but it is also an age in which true life is become possible because of the simplification of the purpose.

The simplicity of the purpose for each of us is that we commit ourselves to Christ. I am His avowedly, His confessedly, and I will follow Him. That is the first and the simple purpose to which I invite every man. Remember that this purpose of loyalty to Christ, formed in the heart and confessed with the lips, is simply the center from which a man is to correct everything else in his life. For Daniel the deepest purpose of all was loyalty to the God of his fathers, and the expressed purpose was his refusal to touch the things that were likely to corrupt that loyalty to God—likely, therefore, to defile him. That was but the beginning of things—the king's wine and the king's meat. There would hardly be a day that Daniel would not have to defend his position and declare his loyalty to God. Some of the youths had to affirm their purpose when Nebuchadnezzar set up his image. The purpose was the same in every case.

I am a little afraid lest I make this thing look complex when I want to make it simple. Purpose loyalty to Christ, affirm it. Then from that center you may begin to construct your circumference and set the externalities of your life right. I meet scores of men who say, "I try, but I fail. I want to be a Christian, but this or the other thing stands in my way." I reply, "You are not to do these things to become a Christian; you are to become a Christian to be able to do these things." Do not attempt to construct your circumference to be in right relationship with your center. Find your center to correct your circumference. We have not forgotten how impossible it is to form a circumference until we have found the center. It is said that Giotto could make a perfectly round *O*. Well, he was the only man who could ever do it, and (forgive the skepticism of this) I have never seen one he made. But I am perfectly sure in the moral realm, in the life you and I have to live, that we shall never make the circumference of life true and beautiful until we have found the center. The first thing is that the man has a purpose in his heart, and that purpose, to crown Jesus Christ. I will begin there, and then, if the king's meat and the king's wine are likely to interfere with my loyalty, I am to refuse and stand upon this central purpose of life.

Daniel Was a Man of Prayer

Nothing stands out more clearly than the fact that Daniel was a man of prayer. When the interpretation of the king's dream was asked, Daniel called his friends together into a compact of prayer and asked them to pray with him that he might have the necessary light for interpretation. As the story moves on, it reveals the truth that he was a man who had regular habits of prayer, who three times a day turned his face toward old Jerusalem, thought on God, spoke to God. Here we touch the secret that underlay his fulfillment of purpose. Strong purpose is powerful in execution only as we are dependent on God. The heart may be firmly determined on loyalty, but unless we know how to lean hard on God the forces against us will prove too much for us. A man meaning to do right and depending on God is absolutely invincible. If the purpose has been formed in the heart, what next? Be men of prayer. What lies beyond the fact of a man's praying? First, his sense of personal limitation; second, his profound conviction of divine sufficiency. What is prayer with these things lying in the background? It is the use of the means of communication between a man's weakness and God's power, between man's limitation and God's sufficiency.

If we desire to live this life in which spirit excels, the life of victory and of power, it is not enough to have purpose. You and I must recognize our limitations, frailties, and weaknesses. In the days of our young manhood, we feel so self-sufficient. When the eye is bright, the step elastic, the will buoyant, we think we can do the high thing, the noble thing, in our own strength. Oh that God may reveal to us at once that this is not so. Sooner or later, the godless life is always a failure and a wreck! Was there ever a man of stronger personality or individuality, apart from Christ, than Saul of Tarsus? Yet he confessed, "When I would do good, evil is present with me" (Rom. 7:21 KJV). He declared that though he willed and purposed the high and the true, in execution he stooped to the low and the false. That is not the story of his high Christian experience, but the story of what he was apart from Jesus Christ. It is the story of every man who has not learned the deep secret of prayer. His own limitation, the fact that the forces of evil about him are too many for him, is one of the deepest and most important lessons any man can learn. "Let him that thinketh he standeth take heed lest he fall" (1 Cor. 10:12).

Side by side with this there needs to be the set conviction of the strength and the sufficiency of God in every human life. Let me put this in the very simplest way so that it may be helpful to some of you. The lot is cast in this great city. Centered in London is every pernicious thing that is likely to blast young life. You have come up to this city, some of you with the great advantages of godly parentage and home training, and some of you have the greater advantage of having been born in the city and of being familiar from childhood with its allurements and its vices. Be that as it may, sooner or later, unless you learn the secret of dependence on God, you will be wrecked and ruined on one side or the other of your nature. I shall never tell you that all you have to do is to realize your own manhood and fight the battle and conquer. I am here to tell you that evil is too strong for you, that the forces that lure are the forces that ruin. In your own strength you cannot overcome. If that were all, I would be silent. But there is another truth—the truth that Daniel knew—the truth that God and Daniel were stronger in combination than all the Chaldean corruption and idolatrous evil; the truth that you and God in London are invincible against all the forces that will sweep against you.

Doubtless I speak to some who have fallen, who have sinned, and they know it. I take you back to the point of your fall, and tell you that your fall was due to your independence. Had you been a dependent soul, trusting in God, recognizing His power, communicating with Him by prayer, always leaning hard on Him, you would have won where you failed. Yet how often young men say, "I have failed and I could not help it." That is partly true and largely untrue. Even if you have purposed solemnly in your heart you will be loyal to Christ, you cannot help failure if you are attempting to fight the battle in your own strength. But if you and I know what it is to trust in God's sufficiency, and to pray, there is no temptation we may not overcome, no advance of the evil one that we may not repulse. Man dependent on God is absolutely invincible. Evil cannot master me if I have attached myself to the infinite resources of God, and if that attachment is maintained by the prayer life. Form habits of prayer. Daniel prayed with his face toward Jerusalem every day. I urge you to have special times, special seasons; I urge you to continue in prayer.

But there is another word about prayer. When Jesus swept away the temple at Jerusalem, He made all the earth a temple for the true worshiper, and not merely in this house or in your own private Bethel, not merely at the appointed moment, but wherever you are, with the eye unclosed and the word unuttered, you can pray. The Puritan fathers talked very much about ejaculatory prayer. I pray God that we may form the habit of it. Realize that when peril confronts you, without waiting for time or place, in the midst of your daily vocation, you can pray. In the moment of such praying the answer of prayer is with you. The great word of the Hebrew epistle is, "We may . . . find grace to help us in time of need" (Heb. 4:16). At the back of that phrase we have a Greek phrase, which we can safely translate by an English phrase with which we are all familiar: "Find grace to help *in the nick of time.*" Right there, when peril threatens, there I may have grace to help. The strong man in London is not the man who says to Jesus in the morning, "I will not forsake You today," and then goes out to fight his battle alone. He is the strong man who says to his Master in the morning, "Lord, lead me today lest I fall," and then prays in the city, in the office, in the warehouse, in the most subtle place of peril, that of loneliness. Everywhere grace to help awaits the cry of the praying soul. Purpose first, and prayer perpetually.

Daniel Was a Man of Perception

Then follow the two results I have mentioned. First is a spirit of perception. There is no doubt that the gift of interpretation that Daniel received was especially bestowed by God for special purposes. The immediate application to us is that to the man who has made his purpose and prays will be given a clarity of vision that will enable him to accomplish the divine work allotted to him. It may be, as in the case of Daniel, that of interpretation, or it may be in some other form. The thing of importance is that the man who has purpose and prays will be of quick understanding in the fear of the Lord. Have you not felt that you need spiritual perception to discern between right and wrong, and that quickly? How often a man says, "I did it before I knew it; I fell before I was conscious of the temptation."

But to the man of purpose and prayer come a growing keenness of insight, sensitiveness of soul, quickness of perception in the commonplaces, and a keen vision in the crises of life. Special illumination from God flashing on the pathway saves him in the moment of his peril. Habits have to be formed, whether they are good or evil. On the basis of purpose and of prayer, a habit of quick understanding of the will of God in matters of life and conduct and a keen insight in the subtleties of temptation come to a man.

Daniel Was a Man of Power

Finally, Daniel was a man of power, first, as we have seen, in small things, but also in great things. I am not suggesting that if you take this position of purpose and maintain it; take this life of prayer and follow it; that if you have this quick, keen perception of God by the Holy Spirit, you will come to a place of worldly power. It certainly is remarkable that this man held office in three kingdoms—Babylon, Media, and Persia. The man of purpose, the man of prayer, the man of perception, was recognized by the men of his age and trusted, and put into places of power, and, as the text says, "the king thought to set him over the whole realm." I am not saying that this kind of promotion will necessarily follow in every case. But I am saying that the man of purpose, of prayer, of perception, becomes the man of power—power that enables him to say no. It is a very old story (you may be tired of hearing it—it was told to you in Sunday school), the story which says that the man who can say no is the strong man. It is still true. Sometimes it takes more courage to say no than to lead an army. The highest courage is not the courage of the battlefield; it is moral courage, the power to say no. I am not giving you an ethical lecture and advising you to say no. I am here to say to you: be a man of purpose, of prayer, and you will be able to say no. What nerves a man to say no in the presence of temptation is the fact that he has taken his stand and is a man of purpose, is a man of perpetual prayer, and, therefore, a man of perception—seeing the issues, understanding the virtues, and able to say no when the moment comes. Our age wants men who are superior to it, not men who are driven by it. Men who are superior to the age are men in whom spirit excels, men in whom spirit has its anchorage in purpose, its source of strength in prayer, its ability to lead in perception, its consequent power in all departments of life.

My last word shall be as my first. For the Christian man, the principle has been focused in a person, so that true purpose is loyalty to Christ, true prayer is communion with Christ along the pathway of life, true perception is submission to Christ and the answering illumination of the Holy Spirit, and true power is cooperation with Christ in the commonplaces and crises of all the days. I pray for you, as I pray for myself, that we may be men of excellent spirit, men in whom spirit is crowned and enthroned, and that we may cultivate purpose and prayer so that we may find what it is to be men of perception and power. The age waits for such men, and wherever they are to be found the result will be that others also will be led into true life.

Joel: Prophet of Judgment

Joseph Parker (1830–1902) was one of England's most popular preachers. Largely self-educated, Parker had pulpit gifts that soon moved him into leadership among the Congregationalists. He was a fearless and imaginative preacher who attracted both common people and the aristocracy, and he was particularly a "man's preacher." His *People's Bible* is a collection of the short-hand reports of the sermons and prayers that he delivered as he preached through the entire Bible in seven years (1884–1891). He pastored the Poultry Church, London, later called the City Temple, from 1869 until his death.

This sermon is taken from volume 17 of *The People's Bible* (London: Hazell, Watson and Viney, 1900).

3

Joel: Prophet of Judgment

The word of the LORD that came to Joel the son of Pethuel. Hear
this, ye old men, and give ear, all ye inhabitants of the land. Hath
this been in your days, or even in the days of your fathers? Tell ye
your children of it, and let your children tell their children, and
their children another generation. That which the palmerworm
hath left hath the locust eaten; and that which the locust hath left
hath the cankerworm eaten; and that which the cankerworm hath
left hath the caterpillar eaten. Awake, ye drunkards, and weep; and
howl, all ye drinkers of wine, because of the new wine, for it is cut
off from your mouth. (Joel 1:1–5)

JOEL WROTE HIS prophecy eight hundred years before Jesus Christ
came into the world. It is a prophecy of judgment. If we liken
ourselves to travelers through this Bible land, we shall feel that
we have come suddenly upon a volcano. *Joel* is a word that means
"the Lord is God." *Pethuel* is a word that means "persuaded of
God." Names were characters in the olden time; now they are
mere lines in a directory. Men were souls in Bible times; today
they are "hands." We know nothing of Joel. He comes as
suddenly and tearingly into the history as did Elijah. His father's
name is given, but there was no need to give it, for nobody ever
heard of it. It is an unknown name; therefore, it stands for
nothing in the history. It is well for a man now and then to come

who has no father, no mother, no ancestry, no relations that can
be traced in so many genealogical lines; a man who stands out
in his own personality, and is all or is nothing according to what
he himself can be and say and do. Such a man is Joel. He has
lips of fire, jaws of iron, a throat of brass. He was a fearless,
resolute, denunciatory man with a gift of righteous damnation.

The word of the Lord that came to Joel. (1:1)

Not the word that came to Hosea or to Amos, but the word
that came to Joel—intimating that there is a word that comes
to every man. "The gospel according to Matthew"—not the
gospel according to John. Matthew could not write with John's
pen; John probably scarcely had patience to read what Matthew had written. They were men of a different spiritual genius. Their gifts were contrastive. Yet each man told what he
saw of the Life, the Truth, and the Way. It was the gospel according to _____, then must be filled in all that is personal,
temperamental, educational, experimental, so that every man
shall tell his own tale and preach his own gospel. The apostle
was not ashamed to say "my gospel"—old, yet new; coming from
eternity, yet accepting the accent of individuality. Each man
has his own view of God, his own kingdom of heaven, his own
way of telling what God has done for him. The mischief is that
we expect every man to speak in the same tone, to deliver the
same words, and to subject himself to the same literary yoke
or spiritual discipline.

The Bible sets itself against all this monotony. Every man
must speak the word that God has given to him through the
instrumentality of his own characteristics. But we have judges
who say they know what they hear. They are not judges of themselves. We cannot hear all the truth until we have heard all the
truth-speakers. We cannot know man until we know humanity. We must know the all before we can know the part. So the
Bible is not to be read in patches and portions, but it is to be
read in its entirety, until part allies itself to part, and strain

follows strain, the whole constituting one massive structure, or, changing the figure, one noble song.

A man cannot say what word has to come to him. A man cannot be both the message carrier and the message origina- tor. We are errand-runners. We have to receive our message and repeat it; we have not first to create it, then to modify it, then to deliver it. The prophets assumed the position of being instruments, mediums for communications that the Lord wished to make with His children near and far, and with the world at large and through all time. Many of the prophets would not have chosen to say what they did. Their message burned their lips; their tongues were scorched with the hard, hot words the Lord gave them to utter. But they could not forbear, they must be faithful. Every word that was told them in secret they had to proclaim on the housetop of history. A man cannot say he will sing his gospel. The Lord has sent only a certain num- ber of singers, and we cannot increase the multitude. No man can say, "I will go forth and thunder the word of the Lord in the ear of the age." The Lord has not given his thunder to that tongue. It was meant to speak peacefully, soothingly, kindly. When it does try to thunder, creation would smile at the feeble- ness of the effort and the palpableness of the irony.

So we have in the Bible all kinds of ministry. There are thun- ders and judgments in the book. There are voices like lutes. There are whispers that you can hear only when you incline your ear with all the intensity of attention. There are words that roll down the mountains like splintered rocks, granites that have been ripped in two by the lightning. And there are words that fall from another mountain as flowers, beatitudes, tender speeches: "Ye are not come unto the mount that might be touched, and that burned with fire . . . ye are come unto mount Sion" (Heb. 12:18–22)—the green mount, the pastoral hill, where God's beauty smiles in God's own sunlight.

But do not let one prophet criticize another and declare that he is not in the prophetic office because he does not speak in this man's tone. Criticism is folly and injustice when it would make all men talk alike and be alike. Let the Lord have some space in His own universe; let Him have some rights in His own household. We have no voice in our own official election. One man cannot be like another man, though he may desire very much to be like some other teacher. When Joel hears David sing, would he not gladly throw away his judgment burden and ask the old minstrel for a harp that he might accompany him in the utterance of his pleading, pleasing, grateful strain of thanksgiving and of joy? But men cannot change places.

The Lord has need of all kinds of men. He wants the fire, the whirlwind, the tempest, the dew, and the still small voice—all are God's ministry, God's husbandry. When will the blue morning dawn—day of justice and of peace and love—when one man shall recognize another man's divers gifts as being as certainly in the prophetic office as himself? When that day dawns, prophecy will have expired, for there will be nothing to predict. The millennium will have dawned and heaven and earth blended in one harmonic identity.

There are others who are sent into the world to upbraid it. It is presumably providential that there should be some upbraiding voices. Perhaps it is presumably providential that some of us have an intense dislike for the ministry of upbraiding. When Christ upbraids, there is justice and not spitefulness in His noble accusations. When other men upbraid, they are apt, under the tone of upbraiding, subtly to conceal somewhat of their own excellence, as who should say, "I never could have done it. Such an action could by no possibility have been done by these fingers. Why did you do it? I told you how it would be. How did you come to run your neck into that noose? How was it that you went contrary to my advice? Did I not tell you?" Oh, cruel tongue! That will never help a man. You never won a man by scourging him so. Do not remind him of what you, magnificent nobody, told him—it was not worth remembering. If the thing itself was good, it was borrowed. Being borrowed, it was spoiled in the delivery. If you can say anything to encourage the man, to give him a new view of his circumstances, to in-

spire him to call up all his fading strength, say it. An upbraiding tongue will turn a palace into a hovel; an upbraiding tongue
can never sing God's music; an upbraiding ministry that is not
instantly followed with healing, encouragement, inspiration,
and ennobling assurance is the worst of cruelty because it adds
to its own venom the hypocrisy of counterfeited religion.

We need ministries of denunciation; we have too few such
ministries. Society is an organized hypocrisy. The denouncer
speaks inwardly, swallowing his own denunciations, and trying
to look benignant where he ought to look like a thundercloud.
Society was never so corrupt as at this day. Joel knew nothing
about corruptness. Eight hundred years before Christ, it was
impossible for men to be as bad as they could be after the Cross
had been set up. From the date of Calvary, all things changed
their relations, that which was formerly venial became henceforth iniquitous, double-dyed in all evil. That which before appeared to be great afterward appeared to be comparatively
small, so all relations underwent modification. No man can be
so bad as a good man. No heart can be so cruel as the gentlest
heart when it is turned in a wrong direction, poisoned and
soured and stung into unwanted animosities. A Christian not
faithful to his Christianity is worse than any pagan ever had it
in his power to be. What can stand before the blasphemy of
trampling under foot the blood of the everlasting covenant? It
lies within the power of men who live in Christian days to be
the worst men that ever lived.

> Hear this, ye old men, and give ear, all ye inhabitants of the
> land. Hath this been in your days, or even in the days of your
> fathers? (v. 2)

The prophets will attend to history; they will not have little or
narrow views taken of Providence. They summon councils of
the old and the young and the many-minded, and they say, "How
stands this fact in the history of the ages?" Fixing our minds upon
locality, we miss the universe. It is possible for a man to be so

devoted a geographer as not to know there is any other world but the earth in all the shining heavens. A man may so belittle himself by his geography as to lose all right to give a judgment on the providence of the universe. We do not understand one age until we have called in all the ages. Today is the product of all the days. This is the advantage of studying history on large lines. This is the advantage of the true university course that takes in all points, all influences, all factors. This is the education that tempers the mind, gives it a new judicial quality, enables it to be cool where minds that have not undergone the discipline fly off into little spasms and sparks of anger and retaliation, not knowing how one thing blends with another and how all things work together in holy edification. So Joel will have a large council, not the young men only, for they can talk but little wisdom; and not any one class, for they know only what belongs to their own relationship. He will have old and young, experience and passion, sobriety and enthusiasm, and he will constitute the whole into judgment.

> Tell ye your children of it, and let your children tell their children, and their children another generation. [And what is to be told? This:] That which the palmerworm hath left hath the locust eaten; and that which the locust hath left hath the cankerworm eaten; and that which the cankerworm hath left hath the caterpillar eaten. (vv. 3–4)

God has many locusts. Only four of them are named here, but they are the greatest devourers that ever fell upon a landscape. They came but an hour ago. They are multitudinous beyond the power of arithmetic to enumerate, and in a few hours not one green thing will be left upon the land. No, their jaws are like stones. They will seize the bark upon the trees and tear it off, and none can hear the crunching of that gluttony. And tomorrow what will the fair landscape be like? It will be like a country smitten by sudden winter. The trees that yesterday were green and fair and lovely will be naked, and their whiteness shall resemble the whiteness of snow. "It is a fearful thing to fall into the hands of the living God" (Heb. 10:31). All the fourfold locust tribe—for all mentioned here are locusts—belong to the Lord. The great providence of God is responsible for its own acts. Man needs to be severely humbled. It does not always suffice simply to bend him a little. Sometimes he must be doubled and thrown down as out of a scornful hand—not that he may be destroyed, but that he may be brought to himself. Soldiers with their sabers and bayonets cannot turn back the beetle. The Lord has made some things so small that no bayonet can strike them, yet how they bite, how they devour, how they consume, how they plague the air, how they kill kings and make nations weak, and turn armies white with panic!

It is easy for philosophers who live in highly rented premises to tell men that all these things are not to be accounted for. Whereas, if a locust could alight upon the head of one of these wonderful philosophers, all his philosophy would not suffice to reconcile him to the painful event. There are no cowards so blatant, so pitiable, as those who say in sunshine, "There is no God. All things have been as they are from the beginning and do not disturb." Let some insect fasten upon the face of these patterers of words that have no juice or wine or music in them, and they will run away from their own sermon and beg to be forgiven for having committed the folly of philosophy. We must deal with facts. Joel knew what he was talking about and could point to the landscape. The locusts came to this place, devoured these grapes, left their signature of death upon these fair fig trees.

We can all refer to similar events. There are parts of our life we dare not look into more than a moment. There were times when our bread was taken out of our hand while yet it was within reach of the lips of hunger. There have been times when our windows have suddenly been darkened. Men told us it was dyspepsia, it was an affection of the liver, it was the weather, it was anything but judgment. Blessed are they who can handle all so-called accidents skillfully and talk of liver and weather and disorder and passing ailments with all the eloquence that is due to such trifles. Blessed still are they, and more, who can believe that nothing happens that has not in it a moral signification, that every touch unfamiliar is a call to attention, because the Lord is going to give testimony to the soul. Rich is that man who finds in his loss a new occasion of praise. Great and princely is he who recognizes in every passing cloud that he is not the master but that the Lord reigns, and the Lord must manage the affairs of His own household.

Awake, ye drunkards, and weep. (v. 5)

Why? The reference need not be specifically and exclusively to wine, though that word is mentioned here. The reference is no doubt to wine and to all narcotics and to all the base alternatives of which corrupt men avail themselves in the time of peril and distress. But the eternal lesson of the exhortation is that all sin ends in stupefaction. "Awake." Are not drunkards always awake? No, they never can be awake in the full sense of the term. Are not all bad men awake, on the *qui vive*, on the alert? Are they not watchful, keen-eyed, lynx-eyed? No, they may boast of being such, but all bad men are stupefied. There is an alcohol working upon them that takes out the brain force and the nerve power and leaves them feeble indeed. Though under some vain hallucination, they may believe themselves to be sane when the mocking spirit of judgment has drawn a film across their eyes and made them see a mirage when they thought they saw a mountain on which was spread a feast of fat things.

All evil stupefies, all wrongdoing takes away brain volume, brain force. Every evil thought robs the mind. Every cruel passion that surges through the blood steals not the purse but that without which the purse is empty. "He that sinneth against me," says the Lord indeed, "wrongeth his own soul" (Prov. 8:36). Suicide is not limited to one act or to one species of madness. A man cannot plot an evil conspiracy without being less a man afterward than he was before. No brain can bear the action of sin without going down in quality, in fire, in fine delicacy, in gift of prayer. He who sins much prays little. He who gives himself up to the captivity of the Devil cares not to look aloft and face the upbraiding stars. All through these grand prophetic books men are called to awake, rouse themselves, shake off their lethargy, and be men in attention and in consecration.

We need a Joel today. For his wages we would award him starvation. He would not live in kings' houses. There is nothing today in church or state that does not need pulling to pieces, cross-examination, analysis, that all that is good therein—and there is much good—may be brought into new cohesion and set to new and fuller uses. Men are bribing men and then going to Sunday school. Many are saying, "If you will get this property on these terms through my hands it will be on the understanding that"—and the all but silent reply is "That will, of course, be understood." And then they go to church! They say, "This is public property, and is not like private property. If I can arrange this for you, the commission will be _____." You understand what I mean. Then they go to some Liberal meeting and shout, "The people forever!" Or to some Tory meeting and say, "Church and Queen!" If some Joel were to come, he would be starved—he must be starved. No one ever came to do messianic work who was not nailed and pierced and crucified.

It is in vain to preach peace until we have first preached repentance. It is mischievous to say, "Peace, peace," where there is no peace. It is iniquity in the sight of God to daub the wall with untempered mortar. Nothing is settled until it is settled at the foundations. A painted cheek is not a healthy one. The true color must come up from the heart and write itself in healthy hue on the face. Having preached repentance, we can then preach peace—we ought to preach peace.

This was the method of Jesus Christ. He began to preach by saying, "Repent." After that came all the sweet gospel of offered love, of sacrifice, of pure doctrine, of noble life. Then came the wondrous mystery of the Cross—Christ being delivered because of our offenses and raised again because of our justification—the mystery of the Atonement, the mystery of Calvary, the ineffable mystery of the Just dying for the unjust that men might be saved. But first there must be Joel-like denunciation, criticism, exposure, and afterward there shall come all that Christ has to say, "Peace on earth, goodwill toward men"—all that Christ can do by way of reconciliation. Until Christ has undertaken the case, we undertake it in vain.

Except the Lord keep the city, the watchmen cannot keep it. Except the Lord build the city, the masons cannot put it up. It is the Lord that does all things, but He must have all His ministers at work—His denunciators, His prophets that fear no face of clay, His singers that know the subtlety and wizardry of music, and His apostles who come with great gospel speeches to heal broken hearts and dry the tears of repentance. It is in the midst of this mystery that we are set. Blessed is that servant who shall be found waiting, working, and watching when his Lord comes!

The Prophet Like to Moses

Charles Haddon Spurgeon (1834–1892) is undoubtedly the most famous minister of the nineteenth century. Converted in 1850, he united with the Baptists and soon began to preach in various places. He became pastor of the Baptist church in Waterbeach, England, in 1851, and three years later he was called to the decaying Park Street Church, London. Within a short time, the work began to prosper, a new church was built and dedicated in 1861, and Spurgeon became London's most popular preacher. In 1855 he began to publish his sermons weekly; today they make up the fifty-seven volumes of *The Metropolitan Tabernacle Pulpit*. He founded a pastor's college and several orphanages.

This sermon was taken from *The Metropolitan Tabernacle Pulpit*, volume 25.

4

The Prophet Like to Moses

The LORD thy God will raise up unto thee a Prophet from the midst of thee, of thy brethren, like unto me; unto him ye shall hearken; according to all that thou desiredst of the LORD thy God in Horeb in the day of the assembly, saying, Let me not hear again the voice of the LORD my God, neither let me see this great fire any more, that I die not. And the LORD said unto me, They have well spoken that which they have spoken. I will raise them up a Prophet from among their brethren, like unto thee, and will put my words in his mouth; and he shall speak unto them all that I shall command him. And it shall come to pass, that whosoever will not hearken unto my words which he shall speak in my name, I will require it of him. (Deuteronomy 18:15–19)

MAN, THE CREATURE, may well desire relationship with his Creator. When we are right-minded, we cannot bear to be like fatherless children, born into the world by a parent of whom we know nothing whatever. We long to hear our father's voice. Of old time, or ever sin had entered into the world, the Lord God was on the most intimate terms with His creature man. He communed with Adam in the garden; in the cool of the day He made the evening to be sevenfold refreshing by the shadow of His own presence. There was no cloud between unfallen man and the ever-blessed One. They could commune together, for no sin had set up a middle wall of partition. Alas, man being in honor continued not, but broke the law of his God. Man not only forfeited his own inheritance but also entailed upon his descendants a character with which the holy God can hold no converse. By nature we love that which is evil, and within us there is an evil heart of unbelief in departing from the living God. Consequently, relationship between God and man has had to be upon quite another footing from that which commenced and ended in the glades of Eden. It was condescension at the first that made the Lord speak with man the creature; it is mercy, unutterable mercy, now if God deigns to speak with man the sinner.

Through His divine grace, the Lord did not leave our fathers altogether without a word from Himself even after the Fall, for between the days of Adam and Moses there were occasional voices heard as of God speaking with man. "Enoch walked with God" (Gen. 5:22), which implies that God walked with him and had communion with him. We may rest assured that it was no silent walk that Enoch had with the Most High. The Lord also spoke to Noah, once and again, and made a covenant with him. Then He, at still greater length and with greater frequency, spoke with Abraham, whom He graciously called His friend. Voices also came to Isaac, Jacob, and Joseph, and celestial beings flitted to and fro between earth and heaven.

Then there was a long pause and a dreary silence. No prophet spoke in Jehovah's name. No voice of God in priestly oracle was heard. But all was silent while Israel dwelt in Egypt and sojourned in the land of Ham. So completely hushed was the spiritual voice among men that it seemed as if God had utterly forsaken His people and left the world without a witness to His name. Yet there was a prophecy of His return, and the Lord had great designs, which only waited until the full time was come. He purposed to try man in a very special manner to see whether he could bear the presence of the Lord. He resolved to take a family, multiply it into a nation, and set it apart for Himself. To that nation He would make a revelation of Himself of the most extraordinary character.

So He took the people who had slaved among the brick kilns of Egypt and made them His elect—the nation of His choice, ordained to be a nation of priests, a people near to Him—if they had but grace to bear the honor. Though they had lain among the pots, with a high hand and an outstretched arm He delivered them. With gracious love He favored them, so that they became for beauty and excellence as the wings of a dove that are covered with silver and her feathers with yellow gold. He divided the Red Sea and made them a way of escape, and afterward set that sea as a barrier between them and their former masters. He took them into the wilderness and there fed them with manna that dropped from heaven, and with water out of the rock did He sustain them. After a while, He began to speak to them as He had never spoken to any nation before. He spoke with them from the top of Sinai, so that they heard His voice out of the midst of the fire, and in astonishment they cried, "We have seen this day that God doth talk with man, and he liveth" (Deut. 5:24).

But the experiment failed. Man was not in a condition to hear the direct voice of God. On the very first day the people were in such terror and alarm that they cried out, "This great fire will consume us: if we hear the voice of the Lord our God any more, then we shall die" (v. 25). As they stood still at a distance to hear the words of God's perfect law, they were filled with great fear, and so terrible was the sight that even Moses said, "I exceedingly fear and quake" (Heb. 12:21). The people could not endure that which was commanded and entreated that the word should not be spoken to them anymore. They felt the need of someone to interpose—a daysman, an interpreter, one of a thousand was needed to come between them and God. Even those among them that were the most spiritual, and understood and loved God better than the rest, yet confessed that they could not endure the thunder of His dreadful voice, and their elders and the heads of their tribes came to Moses and said, "Go thou near, and hear all that the Lord our God shall say: and speak thou unto us all that the LORD our God shall speak unto thee; and we will hear it, and do it" (Deut. 5:27).

The Lord knew that man would always be unable to hear his Maker's voice. He therefore determined not only to speak by Moses but also, ever and anon, to speak by His servants the prophets, raising up here one and there another. Then He determined, as the consummation of His condescending mercy, that at the last He would put all the word He had to say to man into one heart. That word should be spoken by one mouth to men, furnishing a full, complete, and unchangeable revelation of Himself to the human race. This He resolved to give by one of whom Moses had learned something when the Lord said to him in the words of our text, "I will raise them up a Prophet from among their brethren, like unto thee, and will put my words in his mouth; and he shall speak unto them all that I shall command him." We know assuredly that our Lord Jesus Christ is that Prophet who is like to Moses by whom in these last days He has spoken to us. See Peter's testimony in the third chapter of the Acts of the Apostles, and Stephen's in the seventh chapter of the same book. "This man was counted worthy of more glory than Moses, inasmuch as he who hath builded the house hath more honour than the house" (Heb. 3:3). Yet did He bear a gracious likeness to Moses, and therein His apostles found a sure argument of His being indeed the Messiah, sent of God.

The subject of this morning's discourse is the Lord's speaking to us by Jesus Christ, the one Mediator between God and man. Our earnest aim is that all of us may reverently hear the voice of God by this greatest of all prophets. This is the word of God to you this morning, that very word that He spoke on the holy Mount when the Lord was transfigured and there appeared with Him Moses and Elias speaking to Him. Out of the excellent glory there came the word, "This is my beloved Son . . . hear ye him" (Matt. 17:5). This is my message at this hour—"Hear ye him." He says to you all this day, "Hearken diligently unto me, and eat ye that which is good, and let your soul delight itself in fatness. Incline your ear, and come unto me: hear, and your soul shall live" (Isa. 55:2–3). "See that ye refuse not him that speaketh. For if they escaped not who refused him that spake on earth, much more shall not we escape, if we turn away from him that speaketh from heaven" (Heb. 12:25).

Our meditation will run in this line: first, we will think for a moment upon *the necessity* for a Mediator; secondly, upon *the person* of the Prophet-Mediator whom God has chosen; and, thirdly, upon *the authority* with which this Mediator is invested, by which authority He calls upon us this day to hearken to God's voice which is heard in Him.

The Necessity

We begin by considering how urgently there existed the necessity for a Mediator. I need but very short time to set this forth. There was a necessity for a Mediator in the case of the Israelites, first, *because of the unutterable glory of God* and their own inability to endure that glory, either with their eyes, their ears, or their minds. We cannot suppose that the revelation of God upon Sinai was the display of all His greatness. No, we know that it could not be such, for it would have been impossible for man to have lived at all in the presence of the infinite glory. Habakkuk, speaking of this manifestation, says, "God came from Teman, and the Holy One from mount Paran. Selah. His glory covered the heavens, and the earth was full of his praise. And his brightness was as the light; he had horns coming out of his hand." But, he adds, "there was the hiding of his power" (Hab. 3:3–4). Despite its exceeding glory, the manifestation upon the mount of God at Horeb was a subdued manifestation, and yet, though it was thus toned down to human weakness, it could not be borne. The unveilings of Jehovah's face no mortal eye could bear. The voice with which God spoke at Sinai is by Moses compared to the voice of a trumpet waxing exceedingly loud and long, and also to the roll of thunder. We all know the awe-inspiring sound of thunder when it is heard near at hand, its volleys rolling overhead. How the crash of peal on peal makes the bravest heart, if not to quail, yet still to bow in reverent awe before God! Yet this is not the full voice of God. It is but His whisper.

Jehovah has hushed His voice in the thunder, for were that voice heard in its fullness it would shake not only earth but also heaven. If He were for once to unveil His face, the lightning's flame would pale to darkness in comparison. The voice of the Lord God is inconceivably majestic, and it is not possible that we—poor creatures, worms of the dust, insects of a day—should ever be able to hear it and live. We could not bear the full revelation of God apart from mediatorial inter-position. Perhaps when He has made us to be pure spirit, or when our bodies shall have been "raised in power," made like to the body of our Lord Jesus, we may then be able to behold the glorious Jehovah. But as yet we must accept the kindly warning of the Lord in answer to the request of Moses, "Thou canst not see my face: for there shall no man see me, and live" (Exod. 33:20). The strings of life are too weak for the strain of the unveiled presence. It is not possible for such a gossamer, spiderlike thread as our existence to survive the breath of De-ity, if He should actually and in very deed draw near to us. It appeared clearly at Sinai, that even when the Lord did ac-commodate Himself, as much as was consistent with His honor, to the infirmity of human nature, man was so alarmed and afraid at His presence that he could not bear it, and it was ab-solutely necessary that instead of speaking with His own voice, even though He whispered what He had to say, He would speak to another apart, and afterward that other should come down from the mount and repeat the Lord's words to the people.

This sufficient reason is supported by another most weighty fact, namely, that *God cannot commune with men because of their sin*. God was pleased to regard His people Israel at the foot of Sinai as pure. "Moses went down from the mount unto the people, and sanctified the people; and they washed their clothes" (Exod. 19:14). They had abstained for a while from defiling actions. As they stood outside the bounds they were ceremonially clean, but it was only a ceremonial purity. Before long, they were really unclean before the Lord and in heart defiled and polluted. The Lord said of them, "Oh that there were such an heart in them, that they would fear me, and keep all my commandments always, that it might be well with them, and with their children for ever!" (Deut. 5:29). He knew that their heart was not right even when they spoke obediently.

Not many days after the people had trembled at Sinai, they made a golden calf, set it up, bowed before it, and provoked the Lord to jealousy so that He sent plagues among them. It is quite clear that after such a rebellion, after a deliberate breach of His covenant and daring violation of His commands, it would have been quite impossible for God to speak to them or for them to listen to the voice of God in a direct manner. They would have fled before Him because of His holiness, which shamed their unholiness. Because of their sin, which provoked His indignation, and because of the wandering, instability, and treachery of their hearts, the Lord could not have endured them in His presence. The holy angels forever adore with that three-fold cry, "Holy, holy, holy Lord God of Sabaoth."

He could not permit men of unclean lips to profane His throne with their unholy utterances. Oh no, with such a sense of sin as some of us have, and as all of us ought to have, we should have to cover our faces and cower down in terror if Jehovah Himself were to appear. He cannot look upon iniquity, neither can evil dwell with Him, for He is a consuming fire. While we are compassed with infirmity we cannot behold Him, for our eyes are dimmed with the smoke of our iniquities. If we would see even the skirts of His garments, we must first be pure in heart, and He must put us in the cleft of the rock and cover us with His hand. If we were to behold His stern justice, His awful holiness, and His boundless power, apart from our ever-blessed Mediator, we should dissolve at the sight and utterly melt away, for we have sinned.

This double reason of the weakness of our nature and the

sinfulness of our character is a forcible one, for I close this part of the discourse by observing that the argument was so forcible that *the Lord Himself allowed it.* He said, "They have well spoken that which they have spoken." It was no morbid apprehension that made them afraid, it was no foolish dread that made them start, for wisdom's own self in the person of Moses said, "I do exceedingly fear and quake." The calmest and meekest of men had real cause for fear.

God's face is not to be seen. An occasional glimpse may come to spirits raised above their own natural level so that they can for a while behold the King, the Lord of hosts. But even to them it is a terrible strain upon all their powers. The wine is too strong for the bottles. What said John when he saw, not so much absolute Deity, but the divine side of the Mediator? "When I saw him, I fell at his feet as dead" (Rev. 1:17). Daniel, the man greatly beloved, confesses that there remained no strength in him and his comeliness was turned into corruption when he heard the voice of God. Job said, "I have heard of thee by the hearing of the ear: but now mine eye seeth thee. Wherefore I abhor myself, and repent in dust and ashes" (42:5). No, God knows it is not silly fright nor unbelieving fear. It is a most seemly awe and a most natural dread that takes hold of finite and fallible creatures in the presence of the infinite and perfect One. These frail tabernacles, like the tents of Cushan, are in affliction when the Lord marches by in the greatness of His power. We need a Mediator. The Lord knows right well that our sinfulness provokes Him. There is in us, in the best here present, that which would make Him to break out against us to destroy us if we were to come to Him without a covering and a propitiation.

We must approach the Lord through a Mediator. It is absolutely necessary. God Himself witnesses it. Therefore, in His mercy, He ordains a Mediator that by Him we may be able to approach His throne of grace. May the Holy Spirit make this truth very plain to the consciousness of all of us and cause us to sing with the poet:

Till God in human flesh I see,
  My thoughts no comfort find;
The holy, just, and sacred Three
  Are terrors to my mind.

But if Immanuel's face appear,
  My hope, my joy begins;
His name forbids my slavish fear,
  His grace removes my sins.

The Person

This brings us to consider the person of the appointed Mediator, and in my text we obtain a liberal measure of information upon this point. Read these blessed words, "The LORD thy God will raise up unto thee a Prophet from the midst of thee, of thy brethren." Dwell with sweetness upon this fact, that our Lord Jesus was raised up from the midst of us from among our brethren. In Him is fulfilled that glorious prophecy, "I have exalted one chosen out of the people" (Ps. 89:19). He is one of ourselves, a brother born for adversity. He was born at Bethlehem, not in fiction, but in fact. Where the horned oxen fed, He in a manger lay, as any other babe might do, wrapped in swaddling bands and dependent on a woman's loving care as any other babe might be. He was like ourselves in His growth from infancy to manhood, increasing in stature as we do from our childhood to our riper age. Though the holy child Jesus, He was yet a child; therefore, He was subject to His parents.

And when He came forth as a man, His was no phantom manhood, but true flesh and blood. He was tempted, and He was betrayed. He hungered, and He thirsted. He was weary, and he was sore amazed. He took our sicknesses, and He carried our sorrows. He was made in all points like His brethren. He did not set Himself apart as though He were of an exclusive caste or of a superior rank, but He dwelt among us. The brother of the race eating with publicans and sinners, mingling ever with the common people. He was not one who boasted

His descent or gloried in the so-called blue blood or placed himself among the *Porphyro-geniti,* who must not see the light except in marble halls. He was born in a common house of entertainment where all might come to Him, and He died with His arms extended as a pledge that He continued to receive all who came to Him.

He never spoke of men as the common multitude, the vulgar herd, but He made Himself at home among them. He was dressed like a peasant in the ordinary smock of the country, a garment without seam, woven from the top throughout. He mixed with the multitude, went to their marriage feasts, attended their funerals, and was so much among them, a man among men, that slander called Him a gluttonous man and a winebibber, a friend of publicans and sinners. In all respects our Lord was raised up from the midst of us, one of our own kith and kin. "For which cause he is not ashamed to call them brethren" (Heb. 2:11). He was our brother in living, our brother in death, and our brother in resurrection. After His resurrection He said, "Go tell my brethren" (Matt. 28:10). He also said, "My Father, and your Father; and to my God, and your God" (John 20:17).

Though now exalted in the highest heavens, He pleads for us and acts as a High Priest who can be touched with a feeling of our infirmities. God has graciously raised up such a Mediator, and now He speaks to us through Him. O sons of men, will you not hearken when such a one as Jesus of Nazareth, the Son of man, is ordained to speak of the eternal God? You might be unable to hear if He should speak again in thunder, but now He speaks by those dear lips of love. Now He speaks by that gracious tongue that has wrought such miracles of grace by its words. Now He speaks out of that great heart of His, which never beats except with love to the sons of men. Will you not hear Him? Surely we ought to give the most earnest heed and obey His every word.

Moses was truly one of the people, for he loved them intensely, and all his sympathies were with them. They provoked him terribly, but still he loved them. We can never admire that

man of God too much when we think of his disinterested love
to that guilty nation. See him on the mountain there as Israel's
advocate. The Lord said, "Let me alone, that I may destroy them
. . . and I will make of thee a nation mightier and greater than
they" (Deut. 9:14). That proposal opened up before Moses' eye
a glittering destiny. It was within his grasp that he himself should
become the founder of a race, in whom the promises made to
Abraham should be fulfilled. Would not the most of men have
greedily snatched at it? But Moses will not have it. He loves
Israel too well to see the people die if he can save them. He
has not an atom of selfish ambition about him, but with cries
and tears he exclaims, "Wherefore should the Egyptians speak,
and say, For mischief did he bring them out, to slay them in
the mountains, and to consume them from the face of the
earth? Turn from thy fierce wrath, and repent of this evil against
thy people" (Exod. 32:12). He prevailed with God by his pleading, for he identified himself with Israel. Moses did, as it were,
gather up all their griefs and sorrows into himself, even as did
our Lord. True Israelite was he, for he refused to be called the
son of Pharaoh's daughter and cast in his lot with the people
of God. This is just what our blessed Lord has done. He will
not have honor apart from His people, nor even life, unless
they live also. He saved others, Himself He could not save. He
would not be in heaven and leave His saints behind. He loved
the people and so proved Himself to be one chosen out of their
midst, a brother among brethren.

Mark well that, while thus our Lord is our brother, the great
God has in His person sent us one who is lifted up above us all
in the knowledge of His mind. Thus says the Lord, "I . . . will
put my words in his mouth." Our Lord Jesus Christ comes to
us inspired by God. He does not come alone, nor does He come
of His own mind. But He says, "The Father is with me" (John
16:32). "I do always those things that please him" (John 8:29).
"The Father that dwelleth in me, he doeth the works" (John
14:10). Both in word and work He acted for His Father and
under His Father's inspiration.

I beseech you not to reject the message that Jesus brings, seeing it is not His own but the sure message of God. Trifle not with a single word that Jesus speaks, for it is the word of the Eternal One. Despise not one single deed that He did or precept that He commanded or blessing that He brought, for upon all these there is the stamp of deity. God chose one who is our brother that He might come near to us. He put His own royal imprimatur upon Him that we might not have an ambassador of second rank, but one who counts it not robbery to be equal with God and who, nevertheless for our sake, has taken upon Himself the form of a servant that He might speak home to our hearts. For all these reasons, I beseech you despise not Him that speaks, seeing He speaks from heaven.

The main point, however, upon which I want to dwell is that Jesus is like to Moses. There had been no better mediator found than Moses up to Moses' day. The Lord God, therefore, determined to work upon that model with the great prophet of His race, and He has done so in sending forth the Lord Jesus. It would be a very interesting task for the young people to work out all the points in which Moses is a personal type of the Lord Jesus. The points of resemblance are very many, for there is hardly a single incident in the life of the great Lawgiver that is not symbolical of the promised Savior. You may begin from the beginning at the waters of the Nile and go to the close upon the brow of Pisgah, and you will see Christ in Moses as a man sees his face in a glass.

I can only mention in what respects as a Mediator Jesus is like to Moses. Surely one is found in the fact that Moses beyond all that went before him was *peculiarly the depository of the mind of God.* Once and again we find him closeted with God for forty days at a time. He went right away from men to the lone mountaintop. There he was forty days and forty nights, and did neither eat nor drink, but lived in high communion with his God. In those times of seclusion, he received the pattern of the tabernacle, the laws of the priesthood, the laws of the sacrifices of the holy days, the laws of the civil estate of Israel, and perhaps

can cast down their rods and they become serpents, if they yield homage to prophets who call fire from heaven, how much more should they accept Him whose words are matchless music and whose miracles of love were felt even beyond the boundaries of this visible world. The angels of God flew from heaven to minister to Him, the devils of the pit fled before His voice, and the caverns of death heard His call and yielded up their prey. Who would not accept this prophet who is like Moses, to whom the Holy Spirit bare witness by mighty signs and wonders?

Moses, again, was *the founder of a great system of religious law,* and this was not the case with any other but the Lord Jesus. He founded the whole system of the Aaronic priesthood and the law that went with it. Moses was a lawgiver. He gave the Ten Commandments in the name of God, and all the other statutes of the Jewish polity were ordained through him. Now, until you come to Christ, you find no such lawgiver. But Jesus institutes the new covenant as Moses introduced the old; the Sermon on the Mount was an utterance from a happier Sinai. And whereas Moses gives this and that command, Jesus gives the like in sweeter form and in diviner fashion and embodies it in His own sacred person. He is the great legislator of our dispensation, the King in the midst of Jeshurun, giving forth His command that runs very swiftly, and they that fear the Lord are obedient thereunto.

Time will fail us, or we would mention to you that *Moses was faithful before God* as a servant over all his house, and so was Jesus as a Son over His own house. He was never unfaithful to His charge in any respect, but in all things ruled and served to perfection as the anointed of the Father. He is the faithful and true Witness, the Prince of the kings of the earth. Moses, too, was *zealous for God* and for His honor. Remember how the zeal of God's house did eat him up. When he saw grievous sin among the people, he said, "Who is on the Lord's side?" (Exod. 32:26). There came to him the tribe of Levi, and he said, "Slay ye every one his men that were joined unto Baal-peor" (Num. 25:5). Herein he was the stern type of Jesus, who took the scourge of small cords and drove out the buyers and sellers, and said, "Take these things hence: it is written, My Father's house shall be a house of prayer, but ye have made it a den of thieves," for the zeal of God's house had eaten Him up.

Moses, by divine grace, was *very meek*, and perhaps this is the chief parallel between him and Jesus. I have said "by divine grace" for I suppose by nature he was strongly passionate. There are many indications that Moses was not meek, but very far from it until the Spirit of God rested upon him. He slew the Egyptian hastily, and in after years he went out from the presence of Pharaoh "in great anger." Once and again you find him very wroth. He took the tables of stone and dashed them in pieces in his indignation, for "Moses' anger waxed hot" (Exod. 32:19). And that unhappy action that occasioned his being shut out of Canaan was caused by his being "provoked [in] spirit, so that he spake unadvisedly with his lips" (Ps. 106:33). He said, "Hear now, ye rebels; must we fetch you water out of this rock?" (Num. 20:10). Divine grace had so cooled and calmed him that in general he was the gentlest of men, and when his brother and sister thrust themselves into his place and questioned his authority, it is written, "Now the man Moses was very meek, above all the men which were upon the face of the earth" (Num. 12:3). In his own quarrel he has never anything to say. It is only for the people and for God that his anger waxed hot. Even about his last act of hastiness he says, "The LORD was angry with me for your sakes" (Deut. 1:37; 4:21), not for his own sake. He was so meek and gentle that for forty years he bore with the most rebellious and provoking nation that ever existed.

But what shall I say of my Master? Let Him speak for Himself: "Come unto me all ye that labor and are heavy laden, and I will give you rest. Take my yoke upon you, and learn of me; for I am meek and lowly in heart: and ye shall find rest unto your souls" (Matt. 11:28–29). Our children call Him "gentle Jesus, meek and mild." The man Jesus is very meek above all men that are upon the face of the earth. He has His indignation:

Like glowing oven is his wrath,
As flame by furious blast upblown.

He can be angry. The wrath of the Lamb is the most awful
wrath beneath the sun. But still to us, in this gospel day, He is
all love and tenderness. When He bids us come to Him, can we
refuse to hear? So meek is the Mediator that He is love itself,
incarnate love. So loving, that when He died His only crime was
that He was "found guilty of excess of love." Can we be so cruel
as to reject Him? O brothers and sisters, do not refuse to listen
to the voice of this Tender One by whom God speaks to you.

Our Lord was like to Moses in meekness. Then to sum up
all—Moses was *the mediator for God with the people,* and so is our
blessed Lord. Moses came in God's name to set Israel free from
Pharaoh's bondage, and he did it. Jesus came to set us free from
a worse bondage still, and He has achieved our freedom. Moses
led the people through the Red Sea, and Jesus has led us where
all the hosts of hell came overthrown, and sin was drowned in
His own most precious blood. Moses led the tribes through
the wilderness, and Jesus leads us through the weary ways of
this life to the rest that remains for the people of God. Moses
spoke to the people for God, and Jesus has done the same.
Moses spoke to God for the people, and Jesus ever lives to make
intercession for us. Moses proposed himself as a sacrifice when
he said, "If not, blot me . . . out of the book which thou hast
written" (Exod. 32:32); but Jesus was an actual sacrifice and was
taken away from the land of the living for our sakes, being made
a curse for us. Moses, in a certain sense, died for the people, for
he could not enter into the land, but must close his eyes on Nebo.
Those are touching words, "The LORD was angry with me for
your sakes." Words that in a diviner sense may be fitly applied
to Jesus, for God was angry with Him for our sakes. Right through
to the very end our blessed Lord Jesus Christ, our Savior, is a
prophet like to Moses, raised up from the midst of His brethren. O my hearers, hear Him. Turn not your ear away from this
Prophet of prophets, but hear and live.

The Authority

I close with that point, and if my words are very few let them be weighty. Let us think of the authority of our great Mediator, and let this be the practical lesson—hear Him. If our hearts were right, the moment it was announced that God would speak to us through Jesus Christ there would be a rush to hear Him. If sin had not maddened men, they would listen eagerly to every word of God through such a Mediator as Jesus is. They would write each golden sentence on their tablets. They would hoard His word in their memories. They would wear it between their eyes. They would yield their hearts to it. Alas, it is not so. And the saddest thing of all is that some talk of Jesus for gain, and others hear of Him as if His story were a mere tale or an old Jewish ballad of eighteen hundred years ago. Yet, remember, God speaks by Jesus still, and every word of His that is left on record is as solemnly alive today as when it first leaped from His blessed lips. I beseech you: remember that Christ comes not as an amateur, but He has authority with Him. This ambassador to men wears the authority of the King of kings. If you despise Him, you despise Him that sent Him. If you turn away from Him that speaks from heaven, you turn away from the eternal God, and you do despite to His love. Oh, do not so.

Note how my text puts it. It says here, "Whosoever will not hearken unto my words which he shall speak in my name, *I will require it of him.*" My heart trembles while I repeat to you the words, "I will require it of him." Today God graciously requires it of some of you and asks why you have not listened to Christ's voice. Why is this? You have not accepted His salvation. Why is this? You know all about Jesus, and you say it is true, but you have never believed in Him. Why is this? God requires it of you. Many years has He waited patiently and has sent His servant again and again to invite you. The men of Nineveh sought mercy in their day, and yet you have not repented. God requires it of you. Why is this? Give your Maker a reason for your rejection of His mercy if you can. Fashion some sort of excuse, O you rebellious one. Do you despise your God?

Do you dare His wrath? Do you defy His anger? Are you so mad as this?

The day will come when He will require it of you in a much more violent sense than He does today. When you shall have passed beyond the region of mercy, He will say, "I called you and you refused, why is this? I did not speak to you in thunder. I spoke to you with the gentle voice of the Only Begotten who bled and died for men. Why did you not hear Him? Every Sabbath day my servant tried to repeat the language of his Master to you. Why did you refuse it? You are cast into hell, but why did you not accept the pardon that would have delivered you from it?" You were too busy. Too busy to remember your God? What could you have been busy about that was worth a thought as compared with Him? You were too fond of pleasure. And do you dare insult your God by saying that trifling amusements that were not worth the mentioning could stand in comparison with His love and His good pleasure? Oh, how you deserve His wrath. I pray you, consider what this means, "I will require it of him." You who still harden your hearts and refuse my Master, go away with this ringing in your ears, "I will require it of him! I will require it of him." "When he lies dying alone in that sick chamber, I will require it of him. When he has taken the last plunge and left this world and finds himself in eternity, I will require it of him. When the thunder wakes the dead and the great Prophet like to Moses shall sit on the Great White Throne to judge the quick and the dead, I will require it of him. I will require it of him."

My Master will require of me how I have preached to you, and I sincerely wish it were in my power to put these things in better form and plead with you more earnestly. But, after all, what can I do? If you have no care for your own souls, how can I help it? If you will rush upon eternal woe, if you will despise the altogether lovely One through whom God speaks to you, if you will live day after day carelessly and wantonly, throwing away your souls, oh, then mine eyes shall weep in secret places for you. But what more can I do but leave you to God?

At the last I shall be compelled to say "amen" to the verdict that condemns you forever. God grant that such a reluctant task may not fall to my lot in reference to any one of you. But may you now hear and obey the Lord Jesus and find eternal salvation at once for His dear name's sake. Amen.

The Death of Moses

Charles Haddon Spurgeon (1834–1892) is undoubtedly the most famous minister of the nineteenth century. Converted in 1850, he united with the Baptists and soon began to preach in various places. He became pastor of the Baptist church in Waterbeach, England, in 1851, and three years later he was called to the decaying Park Street Church, London. Within a short time, the work began to prosper, a new church was built and dedicated in 1861, and Spurgeon became London's most popular preacher. In 1855 he began to publish his sermons weekly; today they make up the fifty-seven volumes of *The Metropolitan Tabernacle Pulpit*. He founded a pastor's college and several orphanages.

This sermon was taken from *The Metropolitan Tabernacle Pulpit,* volume 33.

5

The Death of Moses

So Moses the servant of the LORD died there in the land of Moab, according to the word of the LORD. (Deuteronomy 34:5)

WHAT AN HONORABLE TITLE! Moses is distinguished as *"the servant of Jehovah."* He was this of choice, for he willed to be the servant of God rather than to be great in the land of the Pharaohs. Such he was most perseveringly throughout the whole of his life. Such he was most intensely, for he waited upon God for his directions, as a servant waits upon his master. He endeavored to do all things according to the pattern that was shown him in the holy mount. Though he was king in Jeshurun, he never acted on his own authority, but was the lowly instrument of the divine will. Moses was faithful to God in all his house, as a servant. You neither see him overstepping his office nor neglecting it. His reverence for the Lord's name was deep, his devotion to the Lord's cause was complete, and his confidence in the Lord's word was constant. He was a true servant of God from the time when he was appointed at the burning bush until the hour when he surrendered his keys of office to his successor and climbed the appointed mount to die.

Oh that you and I may so live as to approve ourselves servants of God! "Unto as many as have received him our Lord

Jesus has given power to become the sons of God," and this is our great joy. But as sons we aspire to serve our Father, even as His great Firstborn Son has done, who took upon Himself the form of a servant that He might accomplish His Father's good pleasure for His church. Let us with good will do service to our Father who is in heaven, seeing it is but our reasonable service that we should lay out ourselves for Him who has made us His sons and daughters. Redeemed from the slavery of sin, let us, as the Lord's freemen, cry unto him henceforth, "O Lord, truly I am thy servant; I am thy servant, and the son of thine handmaid: thou hast loosed my bonds" (Ps. 116:16).

But servant of God as Moses was, *he must die.* It is the common lot of men. Only two have passed out of this world into the abodes of glory without fording the stream of death. Moses is not one of the two. Even had he crossed the Jordan into Canaan, he would in due course have died in the land. We might have expected that he would live on until the people were settled in Canaan. But it seemed right to the Lord God that on account of his one slip he should die outside of the Promised Land, like the rest of the people. Caleb and Joshua alone of all that generation who came out of Egypt were permitted to possess the land toward which they had journeyed for forty years. If that one offense lost him the privilege of entering the earthly Canaan, there may have been still more powerful reasons why he should not enter the heavenly Canaan without experiencing the change of death. He must not make a third with Enoch and Elias, but he must die and be buried.

Such will probably be our lot in due season. It may be that we shall not die. Our Lord Jesus may come before we fall asleep. But if He does not come speedily, we shall find that it is appointed to all men once to die. We shall pass from this world to the Father by that common road which is beaten hard by the innumerable feet of mortal men. Since we must die, it is well to meditate upon the solemn future. Moses shall be our teacher in the art of dying. We will consider his decease in the hope that so our fears may be removed, and our desires may be excited. There is a Pisgah where we must yield up the ghost and be gathered to our fathers. May we climb to it as willingly as did Moses, the servant of God!

The manner of Moses' death is exceedingly remarkable. I suppose that no subject presents a finer field for oratory than the sublime decease of the prophet. But we have nothing to do with oratory. Our object is spiritual and practical profit. Poets might well expend their noblest powers in depicting this strange scene of the man of God alone on the mountain's brow with the view of Canaan at his feet, and himself in holy rapture passing away into the eternal state. We are not poets, but simple believers, desiring to learn some holy lesson from the death of one who, though the greatest of men, knew no higher honor than to be the servant of the Lord. Oh that the Spirit of grace and truth, who has come to us by Christ Jesus, may help us to find instruction in the death of him who brought the law from the mouth of God to men!

Moses Died According to the Warning of the Lord

We are told in the text that "Moses the servant of the Lord died there in the land of Moab, according to the word of the Lord." This I shall read, first, as meaning that Moses died on Pisgah according to the warning of the Lord.

His death was long foreseen. Moses knew some time before that he must die without setting foot in Canaan. Read in the first chapter of Deuteronomy his own account of the sin of the people at Meribah, and the Lord's sentence there and then pronounced: "Surely there shall not one of these men of this evil generation see that good land, which I sware to give unto your fathers, save Caleb, the son of Jephunneh; he shall see it, and to him will I give the land that he hath trodden upon, and to his children, because he hath wholly followed the Lord. Also," adds Moses, "the Lord was angry with me for your sakes, saying, Thou also shalt not go in thither" (Deut. 1:35–37).

His death outside of the Promised Land did not come upon him at all as a surprise. He had to see his sister Miriam, first of

the great trio, fall asleep. Next, he was called to go up to Mount
Hor and disrobe his brother Aaron of his priestly garments,
which he placed upon Eleazar his son. Moses had also to see
the whole of the generation that came out of Egypt with him
buried in the wilderness. The ninetieth psalm is his, and it is a
sort of Dead March. A fit hymn for a nation whose track was
marked by countless graves. Because of unbelief their "carcases
fell in the wilderness" (Heb. 3:17). Only Caleb and Joshua remained, the sole survivors of the great host that crossed the
Red Sea. The Great Lawgiver had thus abundant pledges of
his own departure, and he must have had in his brother's death
a rehearsal of his own. Have not we also had many warnings?
Are we ready?

Concerning his death in the land of Moab, it is natural to
remark that *it was exceedingly disappointing.* He had been for
forty years engaged in leading the people to the land of promise. Must he die when that country was within a day's march?
It was his life's work for which he had been prepared by forty
years in Egypt, where he became learned in all the wisdom of
the Egyptians, and by another forty years in the solitary wilderness, where he kept sheep and held high fellowship with
God. His third forty years had been spent in freeing Israel from
Egypt, training them to become a nation, and conducting them
to the land of promise. Must he now expire before the nation
entered in? What years his had been! What a life was that of
Moses! How glorious was the man who had confronted Pharaoh and broken the pride of Egypt! How tried and troubled a
man had he been while called to carry all that nation in his
bosom and to care for them as a shepherd cares for his sheep!
His was a task that nearly broke him down. Had not the man
Moses been made very meek by the indwelling Spirit of the
Lord, and had he not also been graciously sustained by fellowship with God, his task would have proven too heavy even for
him. Yet, after all that toil in fashioning a nation, he must die
before the long-expected conquest.

It was a bitter disappointment when first the sentence pierced his heart. He had known one great disappointment before, for Stephen tells us that when he smote the Egyptian, "he supposed his brethren would have understood how that God by his hand would deliver them: but they understood not" (Acts 7:25). Then, when his brethren had refused him, he fled into the land of Midian a rejected leader, a patriot whose heroism had brought forth from his countrymen only the contemptuous question, "Who made thee a prince and a judge over us?" (Exod. 2:14). But this denial of entrance into Canaan was a greater disappointment still. To have toiled so long, and to reap no harvest; to see the land, but not to enter it; to bring the tribes to the Jordan's brink, and then to die in Moab after all, it was a grievous disappointment. Are we ready to say as to our most cherished hope, "Thy will be done"? Are we holding our life's dearest purpose with a loose hand? It will be our wisdom to do so.

Apparently, it was a severe chastisement. His offense was but one, and yet it excluded him from Canaan. We have not time to describe in detail the sin of Moses. It would appear to have been a sin of unbelief occasioned by his feeling so intensely for and with the people. Moses was thoroughly knit to Israel. When they sinned, he interceded as for himself. When Jehovah made him the offer that he would make of him a great nation, he declined it solely from his love to Israel. He lived for the nation, and for the nation he died. Remember how once he went so far as to say, "If not, blot me, I pray thee, out of thy book which thou hast written" (Exod. 32:32). In every way he was of the people, bone of their bone, and flesh of their flesh. Israel was hidden in his heart, and out of that master passion of sympathy with the people came the weakness that at last made him speak unadvisedly with his lips.

They strove with God. Though Moses never yielded a point to them in that wicked contest, yet their unbelief so far influenced him that he spoke in anger, and said, "Hear now, ye rebels; must we fetch you water out of this rock?" (Num. 20:10). Then "the LORD spake unto Moses and Aaron, Because ye believed me not, to sanctify me in the eyes of the children of Israel, therefore ye shall not bring this congregation into the land which I have given them" (v. 12). Three times in the book of Deuteronomy Moses tells the people, "The LORD was angry with me for your sakes." It was not so much that which Moses did personally which involved him in judgment, but he suffered because of his being mixed up with Israel. As the Lord had spared the people aforetime for Moses' sake, it became necessary that, when he in any measure shared in their great sin of unbelief, he should be chastened for their sake as well as his own. His faith had saved them, and now his unbelief, being backed by theirs, secures for him the sentence of exclusion from the land.

My friends, when I think of this severity of discipline toward so faithful a servant as Moses, I do exceedingly fear and quake. Truly, "the Lord our God is a jealous God." We are sure that He is never unjust. We are sure that He is never unduly severe. We do not for a moment impugn the righteousness or even the love of our God in this or any other act. But He is terrible out of His holy places. How true it is that He will be sanctified in them that come near to Him! Behold and wonder! That highly-favored servant, Moses, though accepted always in the economy of grace, yet must he come under the rule of the house and feel the chastising hand if he transgresses. Hence, the sentence of exclusion is passed. As he had once joined that unbelieving generation by manifesting a measure of hasty unbelief, he must now share their doom and die on Moab's side of Jordan. "Righteous art thou, O LORD, and upright are thy judgments" (Ps. 119:137). Oh for grace to behave ourselves aright in Your house! Lord, teach us Your statutes and keep us in Your way.

Beloved, *it seemed a great calamity* that Moses must die when he did. He was an aged man as to years but not as to condition. It is true that he was a hundred and twenty years old, but his father and his grandfather and his great grandfather had all lived beyond that age, two of them reaching a hundred and thirty-seven, so that he might naturally have expected a longer lease on life. This truly grand old man had not failed in any respect. His eye was not dim, neither had his natural force abated, and therefore he might have expected to live on. Besides, it seems a painful thing for a man to die while he was capable of so much work. When, indeed, he was more mature, more gracious, more wise than ever. The mental and spiritual powers of Moses were greater in the latter days of his life than ever before. Notice his wonderful song! Observe his marvelous address to the people! He was in the prime of his mental manhood. He had been tutored by a long experience, chastened by a marvelous discipline, and elevated by a sublime relationship with God. Yet he must die. How strange that, when a man seems most fit to live, it is then that the mandate comes, "Get up into the mountain and die!"

Naturally speaking, it seemed a sad loss for the people of Israel. Who but Moses could rule them? Even he could scarcely control them. They were a heavy burden even to his meekness. Who else could so successfully act as king in Jeshurun? Without Moses to awe them, what will not these rebels do? It was a grave experiment to place a younger and an inferior man in the seat of power when the nation was entering upon its great campaign. It would need all the faith and discretion of Moses to conduct the conquest of the country and to divide their portions to the tribes. Yet so it must be. Precious as his life was, the word went forth, "Get thee up into the top of Pisgah: . . . for thou shalt not go over this Jordan" (Deut. 3:27). Even thus to the best and most useful must the summons come. Who would wish to forbid the Lord to call home His own when He wills?

The sentence was *not to be averted by prayer*. Moses tells us that he besought the Lord at that time, "O Lord GOD, thou hast begun to shew thy servant thy greatness, and thy mighty hand: for what God is there in heaven or in earth, that can do according to thy works, and according to thy might? I pray thee, let me go over, and see the good land that is beyond Jordan, that goodly mountain, and Lebanon" (vv. 24–25). This was altogether a very proper prayer. He did not plead his own services, but he urged the former mercies of the Lord. Surely this was good pleading, and he might have hoped to prevail for himself, seeing he had formerly been heard for a whole nation. But no. This boon must be denied him. The Lord said, "Let it suffice thee; speak no more unto me of this matter" (v. 26). Moses never again opened his lips upon the subject. He did not beseech the Lord thrice, as Paul did, in his hour of trouble. But seeing that the sentence was final, he bowed his head in holy consent.

Friends, he had often asked a greater thing than this of the Lord his God. Once he had even dared to say, "I beseech thee, shew me thy glory" (Exod. 33:18), and he was heard even in that high request. The Lord placed him in the cleft of the rock, and made all His goodness pass before him. Yet now he begs for a comparatively small thing, and it is refused. What a mercy that it is in the small things of this life that our requests may be denied, but in the things which touch the kingdom of the Lord our prayer never returns empty! All heaven is open to our bended knee, though for wise ends and purposes a Canaan on earth may be closed against us. All-sufficient grace was given though the thorn was not removed. Moses the servant of the Lord died but triumphed over death.

When I thought of the trial of Moses in being shut out of the land, I found myself unable to read the chapter that lay open before me for I was blinded by my tears. How shall any of us stand before a God so holy? Where Moses errs, how shall we be faultless? Never servant more favored of his Lord, and yet even he must undergo a disappointment so great as a rebuke for a single fault. The flower of his life is broken off from the stalk for one act of unbelief. To be exalted so near to God is to be involved in a great responsibility. A fierce light beats about the throne of God. He that is the king's chosen, admitted to continual relationship with Him, must stand in awe of Him. Well is it written, "Serve the LORD with fear, and rejoice with trembling" (Ps. 2:11). An offense that might be passed over as a mere trifle in an ordinary subject would be very serious in a prince of the blood who had been favored with royal secrets and had been permitted to lean his head upon the bosom of the king. If we live near to God, we cannot sin without incurring sharp rebukes. Even the common run of the elect must remember that word, "You only have I known of all the families of the earth: therefore I will punish you for all your iniquities" (Amos 3:2).

Much more must the elect out of the elect hear such a warning. God did, in effect, say to Moses, "You only have I chosen of all mankind to speak with Me face to face. Therefore, since you have failed in your faith after such relationship with Me, it behooves Me, in very faithfulness and love toward you, to mark your failure with an evident token of displeasure." The discipline of saints is in this life. I doubt not but many a man's life has come to an end when he wished it to be continued, and he has missed that which he has striven for because of an offense against the Lord committed in his earlier years. We had need walk carefully before our jealous God who will not spare sin anywhere, and least of all in His own beloved. His love to them never fails, but His hatred of their sin burns like coals of juniper. Foolish parents spare the rod, but our wise Father acts not so. Walk circumspectly, O you heirs of life eternal, for even "our God is a consuming fire" (Heb. 12:29). The Lord give us to feel the sanctifying power of this passage in the story of the great Lawgiver!

Moses Died According to the Divine Appointment

But now I have to conduct you to a second point of view. Moses, the man of God, died in the land of Moab "according to the word of the Lord," that is, according to the divine appointment.

All the details of the death of Moses had been ordered of the Lord. Time, place, and circumstances were arranged by God. So, friends, it is appointed to us where we shall die and when we shall die. We speak of certain persons as having "died by accident," and we sometimes bewail the deaths of Christian men as premature. But in the deepest sense it is not so. God has

marked out for us the place where and the time when we must
resign our breath. Let this suffice us. That which is of divine
appointment should be to our contentment. We do not believe
in the *Kismet* of blind fate, but we believe in the predestination
of infinite wisdom. Therefore we say, "It is the LORD: let him
do what seemeth him good" (1 Sam. 3:18).

Moses died according to the divine appointment, that is also
according to an appointment that is very general among God's
people. He died without seeing the full result of his life's work.
If you look down the list of the servants of God you will find
that the most of them die before the object that they had in
view is fully accomplished. It is true that we are immortal until
our work is done; but then we usually think that our work is
something other than it is. It never was the work of Moses to
lead Israel into the Promised Land. It was his wish but not his
work. His work he saw, but his wish he saw not. Moses did really finish his own proper work. But the desire of his heart was
to have seen the people settled in their land, and this was not
granted him. Thus, David gathered together gold and silver
wherewith to build the temple, but he was not to build it.
Solomon, his son, undertook the work. Even thus great reform-
ers rise and speak the truth, and cause colossal systems of er-
ror to tremble. But they do not themselves utterly destroy those
evils. Their successors continue the work. Most men have to
sow that others may reap. The prayer of Moses is fulfilled to
others as well as to himself: "Let thy work appear unto thy servants, and thy glory unto their children" (Ps. 90:16). We must
not hope to engross all things. Let us be content to do our
own part in laying the foundation upon which other men may
build in due course. It is according to the divine appointment
that links us with each other that one plants and another waters, one brings out of Egypt and another leads into Canaan.

And I may here notice that Moses thus "died . . . according
to the word of the LORD" *for a deep dispensational reason.* It was
not for Moses to give the people rest, for the Law gives no man
rest and brings no man to heaven. The Law may bring us to

the borders of the promise, but only Joshua or Jesus can bring us into grace and truth. If Moses had given them Canaan, the allegory would have seemed to teach us that rest might be obtained by the Law. But as Moses must be laid asleep and buried by divine hands, so must the Law cease to rule that the covenant of grace may lead us into the fullness of peace.

> Moses may lead to Jordan's flood,
>> But there surrenders his command;
> Our Joshua must the waves divide,
>> And bring us to the promised land.
> Trained by the law, we learn our place,
>> But gain th' inheritance by grace.

Thus, there was a mysterious reason why Moses should die in Moab, according to the eternal purpose of God. Not without such divine decree shall any other of the servants of the Lord depart out of the camp of Israel. We also shall in life and death answer some gracious purpose of the Lord. Are we not glad to have it so? Yes, Lord, Your will be done.

Moses Died According to the Loving Wisdom of the Lord

I have conducted you a little out of the dark now, and the sky is clearing around us. In the third place, Moses died according to the loving wisdom of the Lord. It was a meet thing, a wise thing, and a kind thing that Moses should not go over Jordan.

First, by so doing *he preserved his identity with the people for whom he had cared.* For their sakes he had forsaken a princedom in Egypt, and now for their sakes he loses a home in Palestine. He had suffered with them, "esteeming the reproach of Christ greater riches than the treasures of Egypt" (Heb. 11:26). He had been with them in all that great and terrible wilderness, afflicted in all their affliction, bearing and carrying them in God's name all his days. Was it not meet that he should at last die with them? He had been all along the mirror of self-denial.

Neither for himself, nor his brother, nor his son had he sought honor. He lived only for others and never for himself. His death was agreeable with his whole life, for he leads others to the border of Canaan but enters it not himself. He sleeps with the older nation. He ends his career on the hither side of Jordan, like all the generation that he had numbered when they came out from under the iron hand of the Egyptian tyrant. It seemed fit that one so identified with the people should say, "Where you die, I will die." Are not we satisfied to take our lot with the holy men and women who already sleep in Jesus?

Moreover, Moses might be well content to die there and then since he was thus *released from all further trial.* Surely he had known enough of sorrow in connection with that rebellious nation! Forty years was enough for a pastorate over a people so fickle and perverse. Surely he must have blessed the hand that removed his shoulder from the burden! His was no life of luxury and ease, but of stern self-denial and perpetual provocation. What trial he endured! What self-restraint he exercised! What a lonely life he led!

Are you surprised to hear me say that? With whom could he associate? Even Aaron, his brother, was a poor comrade for such a man. Remember how he failed Moses when that man of God was absent for forty days upon the mount with God. It was Aaron who made the golden calf, and this clearly proved his spiritual inferiority to Moses. The man of God had to watch even his brother who stood next to him. With whom could he take counsel? Who would talk with him as a friend? He dwelt apart and shone as a lone star. It is significant that he died alone, for so had he lived. Aaron had tender attendants to disrobe him. He who put the vestments on most fitly aided to take them off. But the crown that Moses wore, God Himself had set upon his brow and no human hand must remove it.

Surely this burdened watcher of Israel must have been glad when his watch was over! Surely this lonely man, after one hundred twenty years of service, must have felt it a happy release to be admitted to the glorious society of heaven! As Noah was a preacher of righteousness for one hundred twenty years, and then entered into the ark, so Moses, after one hundred twenty years of service, enters into his rest. Is it not well? Do you grieve that the battle is fought, and the victory is won forever? We also in our deaths shall find the end of toil and labor, and the rest will be glorious.

Remember, that by his so dying, in the next place he was *relieved from a fresh strain upon him,* which would have been involved in the conquest of Canaan. He would have crossed the Jordan, not to enjoy the country, but to fight for it. Was he not well out of so severe a struggle? You think of the clusters of Eshcol, but I am thinking of the sieges and the battles. Was it so very desirable to be there? Would Moses really have desired that dreadful fray? Was it not a gracious act on the part of the Commander-in-Chief to relieve from his command a veteran who had already served through a forty-years' war? The Lord would not put upon Moses a burden so little agreeable to his age and to his turn of mind as that of executing the condemned Canaanites. Joshua was naturally a man of war. Let him use the sword, for Moses was abler at the pen. Recollect that the people of Israel were no better when they reached Canaan than when they were in the wilderness. They suffered defeat through unbelief, and they missed much of their inheritance through self-indulgence. Moses had seen enough of them on one side of Jordan without being troubled with them on the other. The Lord, therefore, graciously took his servant off the active list and promoted him to a higher sphere. Let us not be distressed by the fact that He will one day perform the like kindness to us in our turn.

But, you will say, surely it might have been as well if Moses had lived to have seen Joshua win the country. Would this have been desirable? Do active men find much delight in sitting still and seeing others take the lead? Moreover, had Moses lived, he would before long have felt those infirmities from which he had for one hundred twenty years been screened. Is it so very desirable to survive one's powers and to be a tottering old man amidst constant battles? Peace suits age; age agrees not with war's alarms. Had Moses remained the leader of the people, he might have injured the glory of his former days. Have we not seen aged men survive their wisdom? Have not their friends wished that they had closed their career long before? Have we not seen pastors, once able and efficient, holding to their pulpits to the injury of the churches they once edified? Oh that men would have wisdom enough not to undo in their age what they have wrought in their youth! Moses is removed before this evil can happen to him, and it is well.

"But," you say, "perhaps he might have been there to watch with joy the victories of Joshua." Is that always an easy thing to one who has been in the front rank himself? At least, it is not an unmixed privilege. There is a mixture of trial in the blessing. Moses did not "lag superfluous on the stage." He did not survive his work. Who wishes to do so? He passed away on the crest of the wave before any ebb had set in, or any weakness had been discoverable. He died so as to be missed. Israel wept for him, and no man said that he had lived too long. That prayer of his, after all, was a mistake. What would have been the particular joy of merely treading the soil of Canaan? The land looked far more beautiful from Pisgah than it would have done had he stood by Jericho. Assuredly, at the present day, you and I who have never seen Palestine have a much more delightful idea of it than those who have endured its noonday heats and midnight frosts. Moses had more joy in gazing upon it from above than in actually warring among its hills.

Moses Died According to the Grace of God

I must hasten on to say that while the death of Moses thus exhibits the loving wisdom of God, the way in which he died abundantly displays the grace of God.

After Moses had been well assured that he must die, you *never hear a complaint of it,* nor even a prayer against it. Remember, that he himself wrote the story. It is charming to see how he recorded his own fault, his prayer to be allowed entrance into

Canaan, and its denial. Had he murmured, he would have recorded this also. He seems to me always to write about Moses as if he were somebody he had known. He is strictly impartial in his praise or blame of himself. He calls himself "king in Jeshurun" (Deut. 33:5). He says that the man Moses was very meek, and yet he records his outbursts of anger. No man was ever less self-conscious or lived so little for himself as Moses did. Therefore, when once the Lord told him he must die, he acquiesced without a word.

Most fitly the old man immediately *called forth all his energies to finish his work.* You will find in the thirty-first chapter of the book of Numbers that he took in hand a war: "And the LORD spake unto Moses, saying, Avenge the children of Israel of the Midianites: afterward shalt thou be gathered unto thy people" (Num. 31:1–2). He would die warring with Israel's adversaries and obeying Israel's Lord. Certain ordinances to be observed in war he delivered to Eleazar, and he supervised the division of the spoils. Fearing lest the tribes that had settled east of Jordan might excuse themselves from future labors, he stirred up Reuben and Gad and gained from them a promise to go over armed with their brethren until the whole land was conquered. Furthermore, he prepared his manuscripts, not for the press, but to be put away in the ark and to be preserved. He would have his testimony to future generations complete before his hand was paralyzed by death. He knew that he was to die, but he did not sit down and weep, nor sulk, nor give himself up to bitter forebodings of the hour of departure. He served his God with increased vigor and was more than ever alive as life neared its close.

Then he preached his best sermon. What a wonderful sermon it was! How he poured out his heart in pleading with the people! The sermon over, he began to sing. The swan is fabled to sing but once, and that just before it dies. So did Moses at the last give us that famous ninetieth psalm, the song commencing, "Give ear, O ye heavens, and I will speak; and hear, O earth, the words of my mouth. My doctrine shall drop as the rain, my speech shall distil as the dew, as the small rain upon the tender herb, and as the showers upon the grass: because I will publish the name of the Lord: ascribe ye greatness unto our God" (Deut. 32:1–3). Moses had no time for poetry while his whole strength was needed in his government. But now that he is about to die, his frame of mind is ecstatic. Prose will not content him, he must weave his thoughts into verse. In fine, all the faculties of his manhood were drawn out to their utmost in a final effort to glorify the Lord his God. Beloved, is not this a fine fruit of grace? Oh that we may bear it!

Then he gathered the tribes together and blessed them in prophetic words, pouring out his soul in benedictions. Having already cried to God about his successor, he laid his hands upon Joshua and charged him and encouraged him, and bade the people help him in all his service.

He did all that remained to be done, *and then went willingly to his end.*

> Sweet was the journey to the sky,
>   The wondrous prophet tried.
> "Climb up the mount," says God, "and die";
>   The prophet climbed, and died.

> Softly his fainting head he lay
>   Upon his Maker's breast;
> His Maker kissed his soul away,
>   And laid his flesh to rest.

We, my friends, also expect to die. Let us not fear it, but let us arouse ourselves to labor more abundantly. Let us preach more boldly, let us sing more sweetly, let us pray more ardently. As flowers before they shed their leaves pour out all their perfumes, so let us pour out our souls to the Lord. Let us live while we live, and dying, let us die to the Lord. May our life's work close as sets the sun, looking greater when he sinks into the west than when he shines at full meridian height!

Moses Died According to the Divine Favor

Now let us conclude by noticing, in the last place, that Moses died "according to the word of the LORD," that is, according to the divine favor.

His death leaves nothing to regret. Neither is any desirable thing lacking. Failing to pass over Jordan seems a mere pin's prick in presence of the honors that surrounded his departing hours. His death was the climax of his life. He now saw that he had fulfilled his destiny and was not as a pillar broken short. He was ordered to lead the people through the wilderness, and he had done so. There they stood on the borders of their heritage, a people molded by his hand. By his instrumentality they were, so to speak, a regenerated race far more fitted than their fathers to become a nation. The degrading results of long bondage had been shaken off in the free air of the desert. They were all young men, vigorous, hardy, and ready for the fray. It is grand to pass away while there is nothing of infirmity yet seen, nothing left undone, and nothing allowed to fail through too long persistence in office. We may say of Moses, that he did

> His body with his charge lay down,
> And cease at once to work and live.

Moreover, his successor was appointed and was just below in the plain. It was not his son, but it was his servant who had become his son at length. He did not leave his flock to be scattered, his building to be thrown down. Happy Moses, to see his Joshua! Happy Elijah, to see his Elisha! No trembling, for the ark of the Lord mars such a departure. The succession of workers lies with the Master, not with the workers. We are to train men "who can teach others also." But our own special work we must leave with the Lord. Yet as Paul was glad of Timothy, so must Moses have rejoiced over Joshua, and felt in his appointment a release from care.

He died, moreover, in the best company possible. Some men expire most fitly in the presence of their children. Their strength has laid in their domestic duties and affections, and their children fitly close their eyes. But for the man Moses there was no true kindred. You hear that he married an Ethiopian woman, but you know nothing about her. You know that he had sons, but you do not hear a word about them except their names. Their father was too engrossed in honoring his God to crave office for them. As we have seen, he lived as to men, alone, and as to men he died alone. But God was with him, and in the peculiarly near and dear society of God he closed his life on the lone peak. If he suffered a weakness, no mortal eye beheld it. So far as his people were concerned, "he was not, for God took him." Pisgah was to him the vestibule of heaven. God met him at the gates of Paradise.

As he died, the sweetness of his last thought was indescribable. Before his strengthened eye there lay the goodly land and Lebanon. The Lord showed him all the land of Gilead to Dan. Yonder is Carmel, and beyond it he sees the gleam of the utmost sea. Through breaks of the mountains he sees Bethlehem and Jebus, which is Jerusalem. Then, like Abraham, he saw the day of Christ, and by faith beheld the track of the incarnate God. Thy land, O Immanuel, appeared before him, and he saw it in all its spiritual bearings. What a vision! Yet even this melted into a nobler view. As we have seen in our childhood by the light of the magic lantern one view dissolve into another, so did the lower scene gradually melt away into another. The servant of the Lord found himself removed from the shadows that his eyes had seen into the realities that eyes cannot behold. He had gone from Canaan below to Canaan above, amid from the vision of Jerusalem on earth to the joy of the City of Peace in glory.

The Rabbis say that our text means that Moses died at the mouth of God and that his soul was taken away by a kiss from the Lord's mouth. I do not know, but I have no doubt that there was more sweetness in the truth than even their legend could set forth. As a mother takes her child and kisses it, and then lays it down to sleep in its own bed, so did the Lord kiss the soul of Moses away to be with Him forever. Then he hid his body we know not where. Whoever had such a burial as that of Moses? Angels contended over it, but Satan has failed to use it for his purposes. That body was not lost, for in due time it appeared on the Mount of Transfiguration, talking with Jesus concerning the greatest event that ever transpired. Oh that we also may pass away amid the most joyful prospects—heaven coming down to us as we go up to heaven! May we also attain to the Resurrection from among the dead and be with our Lord in His glory!

Soon our turn shall come. Do we dread it? As we are favored to serve our Lord, we shall be favored to be called home in due season. Let us be ever ready—yes, joyfully ready. When we are dying we shall see, not the land of Naphtali and Ephraim, but the covenant. The infinite provisions of its promises will be outspread before our soul, as Canaan at the feet of Moses. Wrapped in happy enjoyment of precious promises, we shall with surprise find ourselves ushered into the place where the promises are all fulfilled.

> There shall we see his face,
> And never, never sin,
> But from the rivers of his grace,
> Drink endless pleasures in.

To the believer it is not death to die. Since Jesus has died and risen again, the sting of death is gone. Wherefore let us prepare ourselves to climb where Moses stood and view the landscape over. Amen.

Jonah: The Unwilling Missionary

Archibald Thomas Robertson (1863–1934) was converted to Christ at the age of thirteen and licensed to preach when eighteen. He was ordained in 1888 but had to resign a few months later because of ill health. That same year, he married the daughter of John A. Broadus, noted homiletics professor at Southern Baptist Seminary in Louisville, and served as Broadus's assistant until Broadus died in 1895. Robertson was named Professor of New Testament Interpretation, a position he held until his death in 1934. The author of forty-five books, all of them scholarly, he is best known for his monumental *A Grammar of the Greek New Testament* and his six-volume *Word Pictures in the Greek New Testament*. He was an effective preacher who used his scholarship wisely and never paraded it in the pulpit.

This sermon was taken from *Passing on the Torch,* published in 1934 by Fleming H. Revell.

6

Jonah: The Unwilling Missionary

Arise, go to Nineveh, that great city, and cry against it; for their wickedness is come up before me. (Jonah 1:2 ASV)

IT WAS IN THE EIGHTH CENTURY B.C. during the reign of Jeroboam II that Jonah lived and prophesied (2 Kings 14:25). Little is told about his life apart from the book that bears his name. No specific claim is made in the story that Jonah himself wrote it. The prayer in chapter 2 is in the first person. We are not concerned with that point, but only with the life of Jonah as there portrayed. The prophets were used of God to stir the people and to warn them of the impending punishment for their sins. Jonah was one of these messengers of God and a very human one at that.

Jonah's Great Mission

"The word of Jehovah came unto Jonah the son of Amittai" (Jonah 1:1). That is an event in the life of any man, even though a prophet of God. It was an event when "the word of God came unto John the son of Zacharias in the wilderness" (Luke 3:2). It demands attention whenever God puts a task upon one's shoulders. The call to you and me may not come by direct inspiration as it did to Jonah and to John, but the path of duty may lie plainly before us, whether the call comes by ordinary or extraordinary means.

In Jonah's case, the demand was that he go to Nineveh, that great city, and cry against it. The wickedness of Nineveh, the greatest city on earth at that time, was rising before the Lord like the smoke belching forth from our modern cities today. There is not a city now that escapes the notice of God, nor a single community for that matter. It is not a pleasant task to cry against a great city to its face. It is much easier to stand off and rail against the vices of the modern Babylons and Ninevehs. Jonah knew that it was a dangerous and an unpopular thing to do that in Nineveh. Nathan did have courage to stand before David and say, "Thou art the man" (2 Sam. 12:7). Elijah was bold before Ahab on Mount Carmel, but he ran like a deer from Jezebel and sat under the juniper tree in despair. There were false prophets in plenty with soft voices and smooth sayings to please princes. Jonah did not relish the call that came to him.

Jonah Shirking His Duty

His heart sank within him at the prospect of facing the great city and exposing its sins. Many a preacher since Jonah's day has had a like experience. It is naïvely said that Jonah got into a ship at Joppa to go with the sailors "unto Tarshish from the presence of Jehovah" (Jonah 1:3). It was as if God did not dwell in Spain. Many a man has gone to the West from his crimes and his loved ones and friends as if God and duty were not to be found out West. But they found out their mistake sooner or later. The eye of God is always upon us even in the dark and even in the haunts of sins. Hugh Redwood has found God in the underworld of London as his wonderful book, *God in the Slums,* shows.

Jonah paid his fare like a man because he was doing what he wanted to do. People, even in emergencies and in time of depression, have money for what they want to do—for chewing gum, for cosmetics, for tobacco, for drink—when they have none for God and His kingdom of grace. Besides, it was a long, expensive, and terrible trip to Nineveh along the edge of the desert with many perils. But it was a lovely sea voyage to Tarshish.

But God saw Jonah all the same and all the time and knew of his willful disobedience. God sent a great wind that raised a tempest and soon the boat was tossed like a ball, and the mariners were afraid. That is always a bad sign when the sailors become frightened. They cast overboard many things. Each sailor called upon his god for help. Plenty of people have no use for God until serious trouble comes, and then they cry to him in terror, a poor sort of praying certainly. But Jonah lay fast asleep down in the depths of the ship. He had gone down there trying to smother his conscience for what he was doing. The shipmaster roused him roughly: "What meanest thou, O sleeper? arise, call upon thy God, if so be that God will think upon us, that we perish not" (v. 6). Perhaps they had heard of Jehovah as God of the Jews. The other gods had all failed them. Jonah had not gotten away from the presence of God. They cast lots to see who was the cause of the peril in which they were. The lot fell on Jonah, and finally he confessed that he was guilty of trying to flee from God and His command to go to Nineveh. They did not know what to do until Jonah himself proposed that they throw him overboard lest they all perish. The men did it with much pleading that Jehovah would not punish them for Jonah's death if he were really innocent.

But God had prepared a great fish, not here called a whale (the word in Matt. 12:40 means sea monster), that swallowed Jonah. This miracle has created a deal of speculation through the ages. Fish have been found with the bodies of men in them, but the men were dead. Jonah could survive in such a place only by the power of God. We have precisely the same problem in the case of Daniel in the lions' den and the men in the fiery furnace. God can do what He wishes to do. Some take it as pure legend. Others regard it as a parable and not meant to be taken as literal history. Jesus spoke of the sign of Jonah as illustrating His own resurrection from the dead (Matt. 12:40f.). Jonah now found out to his sorrow what it meant to disobey God's command.

Jonah Brought Back to God

He was down in the deep waters in the belly of the fish three days and then Jonah prayed to God, a thing he refused to do in the ship. "Out of the belly of Sheol cried I" (Jonah 2:2). He seemed to be in hell itself down "in the heart of the seas . . . all thy waves and thy billows passed over me. . . . The waters compassed me about, even to the soul; the deep was round about me; the weeds were wrapped about my head. I went down to the bottoms of the mountains" (vv. 3–6). It took all this to bring Jonah to a realization of his sins. It takes more than this to bring some men and women back to God. They go so far and sink so low that they defy God. They feel at home in the dens and sinks of shame and have renounced home with all its hallowed ties and defame the very name of God. But Jonah now had enough of his willful rebellion. "When my soul fainted within me, I remembered Jehovah; and my prayer came in unto thee into thy holy temple" (v. 7). At last Jonah is ready to say, "I will pay that which I have vowed" (v. 9). He is willing to go to Nineveh now. He is humbled at last and had plenty of time to meditate. What did it take to bring you back to God when you wandered away? Many a soul has tried to flee from God. Preachers have sometimes fought a call to preach until middle life. God saw that Jonah's heart was now changed and made the fish give up Jonah on dry land.

Jonah Responding to the Call of God

"And the word of Jehovah came unto Jonah the second time" (3:1). That does not always happen. It would not have happened now but for the change in Jonah's attitude toward God. "Arise, go unto Nineveh, that great city, and preach unto ⸮ ⸮he preaching that I bid thee" (v. 2).

The slight change in the language is a direct reference to the first command that Jonah had disregarded and a sharp reminder that he must obey this time. Jonah is willing now and goes "according to the word of Jehovah" (v. 3). He went a day's journey into Nineveh. This street preacher had a short and strange message that must have jarred upon the ears of the people coming from this man of another race: "Yet forty days, and Nineveh shall be overturned" (v. 4). He kept repeating his weird words until "the people of Nineveh believed God; and they proclaimed a fast, and put on sackcloth, from the greatest of them even to the least of them" (v. 5).

This was a new experience for Jonah. Many of the prophets proclaimed God's will to Israel, and the people neglected all of them. Jeremiah, for instance, delivered his long messages through the years to the same people who turned deaf ears to it all. But here the people of a whole city, a heathen city at that, believed the terrible words of judgment and were prostrate before God. The message of Jonah even reached the king who was likewise deeply moved by it. He proclaimed a fast for man and beast in view of the impending calamity: "And let them cry mightily unto God: yea, let them turn every one from his evil way, and from the violence that is in his hands. Who knoweth whether God will not turn and repent, and turn away from his fierce anger, that we perish not?" (vv. 8–9).

The conduct of this king is remarkable from every point of view. He knows better than anyone the violence and evil in his own city, but he refuses to cover it up. Here is a case where the ruler of the city refuses to condone evildoers and calls upon all to turn away from their evil ways. The curse of American cities has been precisely this, that the officers of the law are so often in league with the lawbreakers and for bribes refuse to punish them. The helpless people find themselves preyed upon by the very men whom they have chosen to protect them from the underworld.

Surely no missionary in all the ages was ever so successful in bringing a wicked city to its knees before God. And this missionary had been unwilling to go to Nineveh! And now his message of doom was believed by all, including the king! And yet some men wonder if it pays to send missionaries to the heathen. Does it pay to have preachers at home? "God saw their works, that they turned from their evil way" (v. 10). Here was "reform" with a vengeance. There was never such a cleaning of Augean stables as this. "God repented of the evil that he said he would do unto them; and he did it not." And no wonder. Did ever a city before or since turn round like this? Surely Jonah would feel repaid for coming now when he had saved a whole city.

Jonah's Disappointment at God's Mercy

"But it displeased Jonah exceedingly, and he was angry" (4:1). Instead of rejoicing at this glorious result, he got angry and flew into a rage with God himself. He dared even to justify his former disobedience: "I pray thee, O Jehovah, was not this my saying, when I was yet in my country? Therefore I hasted to flee unto Tarshish!" (v. 2a). So quickly in his anger has he forgotten the experience in the big fish. "For I knew that thou art a gracious God, and merciful, slow to anger, and abundant in lovingkindness, and repentest thee of the evil" (v. 2b). That was the language of impertinence and rebellion against the very character of God. "Therefore now, O Jehovah, take, I beseech thee, my life from me; for it is better for me to die than to live" (v. 3). That is the climax of bitter resentment against the love and mercy of God who had sent him to Nineveh.

God patiently said to Jonah, "Doest thou well to be angry?" (v. 4). Jonah refused to answer. What was the matter with him? He cared more for the vindication of his own proclamation of the ruin of the city than for the lives of the people. He sensitively and foolishly imagined that these very people, whose lives had been spared, would call him a false prophet. He had said that yet forty days and Nineveh would be destroyed and now that was not going to happen. Jonah felt himself put in a bad light with the people. He had rather have his way than save souls. He had rather have his way than God's way. He actually felt himself superior to God. If he could not have his own way, he preferred death to life. He thought he knew better how to run the kingdom of God than God Himself. So soon has Jonah forgotten the storm and the fish.

So in a huff he "went out of the city, and sat on the east side of the city, and there made him a booth, and sat under it in the shade, till he might see what would become of the city" (v. 5). What a picture for us all! There was still a chance that God might destroy the city and vindicate Jonah's preaching. At any rate, he would give God a chance before he finally condemned Him!

God was kind to Jonah as He is to us all. He treated Jonah as a spoiled child as many a preacher has been. He gave him an object lesson. He caused a gourd to grow quickly over the booth to be a shade over his head against the hot rays of the sun. Jonah was exceedingly glad of the gourd vine over his head. Then a worm in the morning cut the gourd and it withered and "the sun beat upon the head of Jonah, that he fainted, and requested for himself that he might die, and said, It is better for me to die than to live" (v. 8). Here he is again upset, this time over a mere trifle and ready to fling his life away for a whim. Then God speaks to Jonah: "Doest thou well to be angry for the gourd?" Imagine the reply of Jonah to the Lord: "I do well to be angry, even unto death" (v. 9).

Some people, like Jonah, become sulky when they cannot have their way in every detail of life. Jonah now, for this second offense, deserved to die, but God was merciful to him as He was to the people of Nineveh. God plainly applies the kindergarten lesson from the gourd to Jonah, who grieved over the loss of the gourd vine. "Should not I have regard for Nineveh, that great city, wherein are more than sixscore thousand persons that cannot discern between their right hand and their left hand; and also much cattle?" (v. 11). There was no answer from Jonah to this telling and overwhelming question. He was silenced, if not convinced. Please note God's pity for the cattle also as well as for the ignorant people of Nineveh, and for the stubborn and willful prophet. Surely we are all wandering sheep, preachers and all. What a call is the story of Jonah and Nineveh to sinners today to turn to God while His mercy still holds out toward us all.

Ahab and Micaiah

Alexander Maclaren (1826–1910) was one of Great Britain's most famous preachers. While pastoring the Union Chapel, Manchester (1858–1903), he became known as "the prince of expository preachers." Rarely active in denominational or civic affairs, Maclaren invested his time in studying the Word in the original languages and in sharing its truths with others in sermons that are still models of effective expository preaching. He published a number of books of sermons and climaxed his ministry by publishing his monumental *Expositions of Holy Scripture.*

This message was taken from *The Victor's Crowns,* published by Funk and Wagnalls in 1902.

7

Ahab and Micaiah

And Jehoshaphat said, Is there not here a prophet of the Lord
besides, that we might enquire of him? And the king of Israel said
unto Jehoshaphat, There is yet one man, Micaiah the son of Imlah,
by whom we may enquire of the Lord: but I hate him; for he doth
not prophesy good concerning me, but evil. (1 Kings 22:7–8)

AN ILL-OMENED ALLIANCE had been struck between Ahab of Israel
and Jehoshaphat of Judah. The latter, who would have been
much better in Jerusalem, had come down to Samaria to join
in an assault on the kingdom of Damascus; but, like a great
many other people, Jehoshaphat first made up his mind without
asking God, and then thought that it might be well to get some
kind of varnish of a religious sanction for his decision. So he
proposes to his ally to inquire of the Lord about this matter.
One would have thought that that should have been done
before, and not after, the determination was made. Ahab does
not at all see the necessity for such a thing, but, to please his
scrupulous ally, he sends for his priests. They came, four
hundred of them, and they all played the tune, of course, that
Ahab called for. It is not difficult to get prophets to pat a king
on the back and tell him, "Do what you like."

But Jehoshaphat was not satisfied yet. Perhaps he thought

that Ahab's clergy were not exactly God's prophets, but at all events he wanted an independent opinion. So he asks if there is not in all Samaria a man that can be trusted to speak out. He gets for an answer the name of this "Micaiah the son of Imlah." Ahab had had experience with him and knew his man. The very name leads him to an explosion of passion, which, like other explosions, lays bare some very ugly depths. "I hate him; for he doth not prophesy good concerning me, but evil."

That is a curious mood, is it not? That a man should know another to be a messenger of God and, therefore, know that his words are true. If he asked his counsel, he knew he would be forbidden to do the thing that he is dead set on doing and would be warned that to do it was destruction. So, like a fool, he will not ask the counsel and never dreams of dropping the purpose. But he simply bursts out in a passion of puerile rage against the counselor and will have none of his reproofs. Very curious! But there are a great many of us that have something of the same mood in us, though we do not speak it out as plainly as Ahab did. It lurks more or less in us all. Dear friends, it largely determines the attitude that some of you take to Christianity and to Christ. So I wish to say a word or two about it.

The Inevitable Opposition Between a Message from God and Man's Evil

No doubt, God is love. Just because He is, it is absolutely necessary that what comes from Him—and is the reflex and cast, so to speak, of His character—should be in stern and continual antagonism to that evil which is the worst foe of men and is sure to lead to their death. It is because God is love that to "the froward thou wilt shew thyself froward" (Ps. 18:26) and opposes that which, unopposed and yielded to, will ruin the man who does it. So this is one of the characteristic marks of all true messages from God, that men who will not part with their evil call them "stern," "rigid," "gloomy," "narrow." Yes, of course, because God must look upon godless lives with disapprobation, and must desire by all means to draw men away from that which is drawing them away *from* Him and *to* their death.

Now, I suppose I need not spend time in enumerating or describing the points in the attitude of Christianity toward the solemn fact of human sin, which correspond to Ahab's complaint that the prophet Micaiah spoke always "not . . . good concerning [him], but evil." The "gospel" of Jesus Christ proves its name to be true. It is "good news," not only by its graciousness, its promises, its offers, and the rich blessings of eternal life with which its hands are full but also by its severity, as men call it. One characteristic of the gospel is the altogether unique place that the fact of sin fills in it. There is no other religion on the face of the earth that has so grasped and made prominent this thought: "All have sinned, and come short of the glory of God" (Rom. 3:23). There is none that has painted human nature as it is in such dark colors because there is none that knows itself to be able to change human nature into such radiance of glory and purity. The gospel has, if I might say so, on its palette a far greater range of pigments than any other system. Its blacks are blacker, its whites are whiter, its golds are more lustrous than those of other painters of human nature as it is and as it may become. It is a mark of its divine origin that it unfalteringly looks facts in the face and will not say smooth things about men as they are.

Side by side with that characteristic of the dark picture that it draws of us, as we are of ourselves, is its unhesitating restraint or condemnation of deep-seated desires and tendencies. It does not come to men with the smooth words on its lips, "Do as you will." It does not seek for favor by relaxing bonds, but it rigidly builds up a wall on either side of a narrow path and says, "Walk within these limits and you are safe. Go beyond them a hair's-breadth, and you perish." It may suit Ahab's prophets to fling the reins on the neck of human nature; God's prophet says, "You shall not." That is another of the tests of divine origin, that there shall be no base compliance with inclinations but rigid condemnation of many of our deep desires.

Side by side with these two characteristics is a third characteristic that the Word, which is the outcome and expression of
the divine love, is distinguished by its plain and stern declara-
tions of the bitter consequences of evildoing. I need not dwell
upon these. They seem to me to be far too solemn to be spoken of by a man to men in words other than Scripture's. But I
beseech you to remember that this, too, is the characteristic of
Christ's message. So a man may say, when he thinks of the dark
and solemn things that the Old Testament partially, and the
New Testament more clearly, utter as to the death that is the
outcome of sin, that these are indeed the very voice of infinite
love pleading with us all. Do not so misapprehend facts as to
think that the restraints, threatenings, and dark pictures that
Christ and His servants have drawn are anything but the utterance of the purest affection.

The Strange Dislike That This Attitude of Christianity Kindles

I have said that Ahab's mental condition was a very odd one.
As strange as it is, it is, as I have already remarked, in some
degree a very frequent one. There are in us all, as we see in
many regions of life, the beginnings of the same kind of feeling. Here, for example, is a course that I am quite sure, if I
pursue it, will land me in evil. Does the drunkard take a glass
less because he knows that if he goes on he will have a
drunkard's liver and die a miserable death? Does the gambler
ever take away his hand from the pack of cards or the dice box
because he knows that play means, in the long run, poverty
and disgrace? When a man sets his will upon a certain course,
he is like a bull that has started in its rage. Down goes the head,
and, with eyes shut, he will charge a stone wall or an iron door,
though he knows it will smash his skull. Men are very foolish
animals. There is no greater mark of their folly than the con-
spicuous and often repeated fact that the clearest vision of the
consequences of a course of conduct is powerless to turn a man
from it, when once his passions or his will or, worse still, his
weakness or, worst of all, his habits have bound him to it.

Take another illustration. Do we not all know that honest friends have sometimes fallen out of favor, perhaps with ourselves, because they have persistently kept telling us what our consciences and common sense knew to be true—that if we go on by that road we shall be suffocated in a bog? A man makes up his mind to a course of conduct. He has a shrewd suspicion that his honest friend will condemn it and that the condemnation will be right. What does he do, therefore? He never tells his friend, and if by chance that friend should say what was expected of him, he gets angry with his adviser and goes his road. I suppose we all know what it is to treat our consciences in the style in which Ahab treated Micaiah. We do not listen to them because we know what they will say before they have said it. We call ourselves sensible people! Martin Luther once said, "It is neither safe nor wise to do anything against conscience." But Ahab put Micaiah in prison. We shut up our consciences in a dungeon, put a gag in their mouths and a muffler over the gag that we may hear them say no word because we know that what we are doing—and we are doggedly determined to do—is wrong.

But the saddest illustration of this infatuation is to be found in the attitude that many men take in regard to Christianity. There is a great craving today, more perhaps than there has been in some other periods of the world's history, for a religion that shall adorn but shall not restrain. People are looking for a religion that shall be toothless and have no bite in it. They want a religion that shall sanction anything that it pleases our sovereign mightiness to want to do. We should all like to have God's sanction for our actions. But there are a great many of us that will not take the only way to secure that—that is, to do the actions that He commands and to abstain from those that He forbids. Popular Christianity is a very easy-fitting garment. It is like an old shoe that you can slip off and on without any difficulty. But a religion that does not put up a strong barrier between you and many of your inclinations is not worth anything. The mark of a message from God is that it restrains and coerces and forbids and commands. And some of you do not like it because it does.

There is a great tendency in this day to cut out of the Old and New Testaments all the pages that say things like this, "The soul that sinneth, it shall die" (Ezek. 18:4, 20); or things like this, "This is the condemnation, that light is come into the world, and men love darkness rather than light" (John 3:19). Friends, men being what they are, and God being what He is, there can be no divine message without a side of what the world calls threatening or what Ahab called "prophesying evil." I beseech you, do not be carried away by the modern talk about Christianity being gloomy and dark or fancy that it is a blot and an excrescence upon the pure religion of the Man of Nazareth when we speak of the death that follows sin and of the darkness into which unbelief carries a man.

The Intense Folly of Such an Attitude

Ahab hated Micaiah. Why? Because Micaiah told him what would come to him as the fruit of his own actions. That was foolish. It is no less foolish for people to take up a position of dislike and to turn away from the gospel of Jesus Christ because it speaks in like manner. I said that men are very foolish animals. There is surely nothing in all the annals of human stupidity more stupid than to be angry with the Word that tells you the truth about what you are bringing down upon your heads. It is absurd because Micaiah did not make the evil, but Ahab made it. Micaiah's business was only to tell him what he was doing. It is absurd because the only question to be asked is, Are the warnings true? Are the threatenings representations of what really will come? Are the prohibitions reasonable? And it is absurd, because if these things are so—if it is true that the soul that sins dies and will die; if it is true that you who have heard the name and the salvation of Jesus Christ over and over again and have turned away from it will, if you continue in that negligence and unbelief, reap bitter fruits here and hereafter therefrom—if these things are true, surely the man that tells you and the gospel that tells you deserve better treatment than Ahab's petulant hatred or your stolid indifference and neglect.

Would you think it wise for a sea captain to try to take the clapper out of the bell that floats and tolls above a shoal on which his ship will be wrecked if it strikes? Would it be wise to put out the lighthouse lamps and then think that you had abolished the reef? Does the signalman with his red flag make the danger of which he warns? And is it not like a baby to hate and to neglect the message that comes to you and says, "Turn, turn, why will you die?"

The End of This Foolish Attitude

Ahab was told in plain words by Micaiah, before the interview closed, that he would never come back again in peace. He ordered the bold prophet into prison and rode away happily, no doubt, to his campaign. Weak men are very often obstinate because they are not strong enough to rise to the height of changing a purpose when reason urges. This weak man was always obstinate in the wrong place, as so many of us are. So away he went, down from Samaria, across the plain, down to the fords of the Jordan. But when he had crossed to the other side and was coming near his objective point, the memories of Micaiah in prison at Samaria began to sit heavy on his soul.

So he tried to dodge divine judgment and got up an ingenious scheme by which his ally was to go into the field in royal pomp and he to slip into it disguised. A great many of us try to dodge God, and it does not answer. The man who "drew a bow at a venture" (1 Kings 22:34; 2 Chron. 18:33) had his hand guided by a higher hand. Ahab was plated all over with iron and brass, but there is always a crevice through which God's arrow can find its way. Where God's arrow finds its way, it kills. When the night fell, he was lying dead on his chariot floor, the host was scattered, and Micaiah, the prisoner, was avenged. His word took hold on the despiser of it.

So it always will be. So it will be with us, dear friends, if we do not take heed to our ways and listen to the Word which may be bitter in the mouth, but, taken, turns sweet as honey. Nailing the index of the barometer to "set fair" will not keep off the thunderstorm, and no negligence or dislike of divine threatenings will arrest the slow, solemn march, inevitable as destiny, of the consequence of our doings. Things will be as they will be; believed or unbelieved, the avalanche will come.

Dear friends, there is one way to get Micaiah on our side. Listen to him, and then he will speak good to you and not what you foolishly call evil. Let God's Word convince you of sin. Let it bring you to the Cross for pardon. Jesus Christ addresses each of us in the apostle's words: "Am I therefore become your enemy, because I tell you the truth?" (Gal. 4:16). The sternest "threatenings" in the Bible come from the lips of that infinite Love. If you will listen to Him, if you will yield yourselves to Him, if you will take Him for your Savior and your Lord, if you will cast your confidence and anchor your love upon Him, if you will let Him restrain you, if you will consult Him about what He would have you do, if you will accept His prohibitions as well as His permissions, then His Word and His act to you, here and hereafter, will be only good and not evil all the days of your life.

Remember Ahab lying dead on the floor of his chariot in a pool of his own blood, and think for yourselves of what despising the threatenings and turning away from the rebukes and prohibitions of the divine Word come to. These threatenings are spoken that they may never need to be put into effect. If you give heed to them, they will never be put into effect in regard to you. If you choose to neglect them and "will none of" God's "reproof," they will come down on you like a mighty rock loosened from the mountain and will grind you to powder.

Nathan: Preacher to a King

Clarence Edward Noble Macartney (1879–1957) ministered in Paterson, New Jersey, and Philadelphia, Pennsylvania, before assuming the influential pastorate of First Presbyterian Church, Pittsburgh, Pennsylvania, where he ministered for twenty-seven years. His preaching especially attracted men, not only to the Sunday services but also to his popular Tuesday noon luncheons. He was gifted in dealing with Bible biographies and, in this respect, has been called "the American Alexander Whyte." Much of his preaching was topical-textual, but it was always biblical, doctrinal, and practical. Perhaps his most famous sermon is "Come Before Winter."

The sermon I have selected was taken from *The Woman of Tekoah, and Other Sermons,* published by Cokesbury Press in 1938.

8

Nathan: Preacher to a King

And the LORD sent Nathan. (2 Samuel 12:1)

WHEN MAN SENDS HIMSELF, or sends another man, no startling results are to be expected. But when God sends a man, then great things will happen. "There was a man sent from God, whose name was John." Here is another man sent from God, whose name was Nathan.

Nathan was one of the six chief actors in one of the most moving, most terrible, saddest, most alarming tragedies of the Bible, a book full of stirring, moving, and dramatic events. These are the six chief actors: David, the king; Uriah the Hittite; Bathsheba, his wife; the child born to David and Bathsheba; Joab, David's commander-in-chief; and Nathan the prophet. And then there was the supreme Actor Himself, God. What a drama this is! Genius, royalty, temptation, sin, conscience, hypocrisy, cruelty, murder; a brokenhearted mother anointing her dying babe with unavailing tears; a father agonizing in prayer; a loyal and heroic soldier treacherously done to death; a great preacher and a great sermon; retribution, repentance, and forgiveness. Where, in or out of the Bible, can it be matched?

That so terrible a chapter appears in the Bible, and in the history of one of the Bible's chief characters, is a proof of the

divine origin of the Bible. What forger or impostor pretend-
ing to write an inspired book would have inserted such a record
of sin and shame concerning David, spoken of elsewhere as a
man after God's heart? If this story appears in the Bible, it is
because God put it there.

David's First Fall

A student of literature made it a custom to read through
Shakespeare's *Macbeth* once every year so that he might warn
his soul against the peril that lurks in the pool of imagination
and desire, for that tragedy shows how the once loyal and faithful Macbeth became an assassin and murderer. But if one reads
the Bible, there is no need of reading Shakespeare or any other
literature for warning against sin. Suffice it to say that David
was a man of like passions with us. If this happened to the man
who wrote the twenty-third psalm and the ninety-first psalm,
then who of us will consider himself above warning?

Some have scoffed at David's being called a man "after
[God's] heart" (see Acts 13:22). But this description was written of David long before his fall and in contrast with Saul, and
also long after his fall in connection with Jeroboam, the son of
Nebat, who made Israel to sin. In contrast with either king,
David was indeed a man after God's heart—one who desired
to do the will of God. How many noble traits he had! He was
just, magnanimous, and devout. He was deeply affectionate as
a father, weeping alike over the death of the little babe—the
child of his sin—and over Absalom, who drove him from his
throne and sought to kill him. David was also ever thankful,
too, calling upon his soul and all that was within him to bless
the Lord and forget not all His benefits. Out of his trials, joys,
sorrows, temptations, sins, forgiveness, and restoration, David
composed and sang those psalms and songs that, until they shall
blend with the angels' songs in heaven, echo all the music of
man's soul.

Everybody loved David. If such a man fell into this temptation and sin, his fall locates for us that abyss which yawns ever

near to the gates of genius and devotion, as in *Pilgrim's Progress* there was an opening to the pit of hell hard by the gate of the Celestial City.

The natural history and sequence of temptation and sin is clearly stated by James: "Every man is tempted, when he is drawn away of his own lust, and enticed. Then when lust hath conceived, it bringeth forth sin: and sin, when it is finished, bringeth forth death" (James 1:14). Lay these verses alongside the chapter of 2 Samuel that tells of David's fall and the consequence of it, and the two passages—James's principle and theory of sin and David's history in temptation and sin—fit exactly one into the other.

David's fall looks like a sudden fall, but there is always a preparation for such a fall. On an autumn day going through the woods, you put your foot down upon a fallen log and immediately it gives way, for the log is rotten. Its collapse is sudden, but months and years of summer rains and winter snows have slowly been corrupting the log and causing it to disintegrate and decay. The Johnstown dam gave way with a roar and crash in a moment of time on that May day in 1889, and two thousand perished in the raging torrent. But for weeks and months the waters imprisoned by the dam had slowly, unobservedly been eroding the wall of the dam. So it is with moral disasters. There must have been something in David's history before this fall that was preparing the way for it.

The power of temptation depends upon the mood and state of mind in which temptation finds the soul. Jesus said that Satan came to him and found nothing in Him. He came to David that fateful evening when David, walking on his roof garden, saw Bathsheba at her bath and found much in him. The door had been left open. David had seen many beautiful women before this and under various circumstances but not with the results of this vision. Hence, the necessity of guarding the pool of imagination and desire and resisting temptation at its first on set. If a spark falls on marble or ice, nothing happens; it merely goes out. But if the same spark falls on the powder magazine, there is combustion, explosion, and death. So temptation finds the unguarded heart. It was not for nothing that Jesus said, "Watch and pray, that ye enter not into temptation" (Matt. 26:41).

As for David's state of heart on the day of his temptation, all we know is that he had passed through his trials and dangers and his long wait and probation for the throne of Israel. He had been crowned king; Saul's house was fallen. God had blessed David with victory and prosperity, and his name and fame were spread abroad in the earth. Perhaps that had something to do with his fall. Prosperity has its perils. After David, one of the greatest kings of Judah was Uzziah, a great organizer, builder, soldier, and administrator. His kingdom reached a degree of power and splendor that it had not known before or after him. Yet the great king Uzziah died an outcast and a leper in the lazar house. And why? This is the record: "But when he was strong, his heart was lifted up to his destruction: for he transgressed against the LORD his God" (2 Chron. 26:16).

When David inquired who the woman was whom he had seen from his balcony, he learned that she was the wife of Uriah the Hittite, one of his soldiers then at the front at the siege of the Ammonite stronghold, Rabbah. Through his valor and courage in battle, Uriah had risen to high distinction, for he is named as one of David's thirty-two mighty men. The fact that Bathsheba was the wife of this faithful and courageous officer ought of itself to have given David pause for thought, for the king was the protector of his people, and Uriah was risking his life for his king. Notwithstanding, David took the next step into sin and sent for Bathsheba.

David's Second Fall

What followed the first transgression was far worse than what had gone before. The first sin was one of passion and impulse. But now came two diabolical plots, both hypocritical and shameful. Oriental kings were accustomed to do as they pleased. But David was not just an oriental king, he was the king of Israel.

He knew the commandments of God and knew that he had broken one of them. He knew also the law of the land. For the sake of his honor and reputation, and perhaps because he feared for his life, David tried to save himself from exposure by making it appear that Uriah was the father of the child who would be born. He sent a command to Joab, leading the army against Rabbah, to send Uriah the Hittite to him at Jerusalem.

Joab probably wondered what David wanted of Uriah. Uriah too must have wondered as he left the camp and came to Jerusalem. Perhaps he thought that David had become suspicious of his Hittite origin, for the Hittites were a people accursed to Israel. Or he may have thought that someone had been slandering him to the king. But when he arrived at the palace, he was at once relieved of his fears, for David greeted him kindly and said to him, "How goes the battle at Rabbah? Are the soldiers of the army in good spirits and in good health?" When Uriah reported how things stood with the army in the campaign against the Ammonites, David said to him, "I am going to give you a brief furlough, for you are one of my most valiant and trusted officers. Would I had more like you! You well deserve a place in my thirty-two mighty men. Go down to your home, visit with your wife, and have a good rest before you return to the front."

Had Uriah gotten word of what had happened? Was he suspicious of David's motive in sending him down to his house for a rest? No, I think not. But so high was his sense of a soldier's duty that, instead of going down to his house, he slept in the guard room with the king's bodyguard. When David learned this in the morning, he summoned Uriah and inquired of him why he had not availed himself of the royal kindness and rested at his own home, instead of sleeping with the guard. The answer of the noble-minded and loyal Uriah was that when his fellow officers and soldiers were sleeping in the open fields and in the trenches, he did not feel it was proper for him to take his ease at home.

Now David sank still lower. He had failed with Uriah sober;

perhaps he could succeed with Uriah drunk. He invited Uriah to spend another day at the palace and had him eat and drink with him at the king's table. In the long history of strong drink there can be found no stronger indictment of it and its power to suspend man's reason and rouse his passions than what we are told here. David plied Uriah with drink until that courageous soldier became drunk. But instead of going to his home when he staggered away from the royal board, he fell down in the guard room and slept again with David's bodyguard.

Now David was desperate. Having failed to foist the paternity of the child upon the husband of the woman, he resolved to slay Uriah, for Uriah dead would not be able to say that the child was not his. In all the known annals of ancient courts, and in all records of wicked kings and nobles, and of murders and assassinations, there can be found nothing worse than the story of the murder of Uriah. The time was short. Uriah must die!

If David had slain Uriah with his own sword or ordered one of his bodyguards to do so or commanded Joab to put him to death on some trumped-up charge, that would have been bad enough. But instead of that, David plotted to have Uriah killed in the midst of the battle and fall at the hand of the enemy in the line of duty. To accomplish this, he wrote a letter to Joab. This is the first letter mentioned in Bible history and the worst in all history. He sent the letter to Joab by the hand of Uriah, who little dreamed that he was carrying his own death warrant. In the letter David ordered Joab to make an assault upon the Ammonites and to set Uriah in the forefront of the hottest battle. Then Joab and all others in the attacking party were suddenly to withdraw and leave Uriah alone, so that he would be smitten and die.

Joab carried out this cruel and shameful order. When the trumpets sounded for the attack, Uriah was assigned a place in the van "where valiant men liked to be" (see 2 Sam. 11:16). At a given signal from Joab, the soldiers fighting by the side of Uriah fell back, but Uriah knew it not, for his eyes were on the foe. On he fought, all alone, smiting down one foe after another, for he was worthy of his place among the thirty-two mighty men. So fighting he fell. Perhaps his last thoughts were for his wife and for his king. When he died the hero's death on the field of battle, Uriah never dreamed that it was not the sword of an Ammonite that had slain him but the sword of David his king.

Joab now played his own hypocritical part and pretended to make a formal report to David. The messenger was to tell David of the assault against Rabbah and the repulse of the attacking force. If David showed displeasure and asked why they came so near to the wall in the battle, and mentioned the fate of Abimelech, Gideon's son, who was slain by a millstone that a woman hurled down on him from the wall when he was attacking Thebez, the messenger was to say to the king that Uriah was among those killed in the battle.

The messenger delivered his message. But, contrary to his expectations, David displayed no displeasure, but in a masterpiece of duplicity told the runner to tell Joab not to be cast down by the repulse and the death of Uriah, "for the sword devoureth one as well as another" (v. 25). I wonder if grim Joab smiled when he received that condolence from David. When Bathsheba heard of the death of her husband, she mourned for him seven days. "When the mourning was past, David sent and fetched her to his house, and she became his wife" (27a). "All is well," thought David to himself. "I will give Uriah the burial that a hero deserves. None knows how he came to die, save Joab, and I can count on him not to tell."

Then comes one of the masterpieces of the Bible—the sole comment of the inspired historian on David's dastardly deed. But what a comment it is: "But the thing that David had done displeased the LORD" (27b). Forever this brief sentence dismisses the thought that God was indifferent to what David had done. The great historian of the books of Samuel, like Othello, "nothing extenuates, nor aught sets down in malice." All that he does is to relate the facts. Among the facts is this last fact: "The thing that David had done displeased the LORD." Do you ever think of that? That your every deed and every thought either pleases or displeases God?

Nathan's Sermon and David's Repentance

Almost a year had passed, but David showed no sign of repentance. We would like to look into David's heart during that year. Sin, once committed, has great blinding and enslaving power. Sin always looks worse in others than in ourselves. No doubt David sought excuses for his heinous sin. Perhaps when that death's head appeared at the banqueting table, or looked upon him from the foot of the royal couch, David exclaimed, "No; it was not I that slew him. Not I; but the sword of Israel's bitter and accursed foe, the Ammonite. Uriah was not murdered. Uriah died in battle for Israel."

It is impossible to think that a man who had enjoyed such fellowship with God and such favor from God's hand could rest at ease after this infamous deed. No; I am sure there were times when David took up his harp to play but found it so badly out of tune because his soul was out of tune with God that he flung it down, and, pacing to and fro on his roof garden, cried aloud, "Would to God that I had never come on this roof that fatal night! Would God that, like Job, I had made a covenant with mine eyes not to think upon a maid!" When all is wrong within a man's heart, the internal distress sometimes will show itself in acts of severity and cruelty. This was so in the case of David. It was after his great sin and before his repentance that David's army under Joab took Rabbah, where Uriah had fallen in battle. Contrary to his usual magnanimity, David treated the inhabitants with great cruelty, torturing them with saws and harrows of iron. When David went to the front, Joab gave him the heavy crown studded with precious stones, which the king of the Ammonites had worn on his head, and set it on David's head. But, alas, David, although you wear the beautiful crown of the conquered king of Ammon, you have discrowned yourself by your sin!

But whatever David's inner distress and remorse, there was

no repentance and no confession. Then the Lord sent Nathan to David. This was not the first nor the last time that a man of God was sent of God to rebuke a king, and, although his life was at stake, Nathan was true to his office. Samuel was sent to rebuke Saul for his folly and to tell him that God would rend the kingdom from him and give it to David. Moses was sent to rebuke Pharaoh. Elijah was sent with his "thus saith the Lord" to wicked Ahab and bloodthirsty Jezebel. John the Baptist was sent to rebuke Herod Antipas and his paramour, Herodias. Ambrose, the bishop of Milan, was sent to rebuke the emperor Theodosius for his massacre of citizens at Thessalonica, forbidding him to enter the church or receive the sacrament. When Theodosius reminded him that David too was a great sinner, Ambrose answered, "You have imitated David in his sins; now imitate him in his repentance."

Never did a man of God have a more difficult message to deliver. Nathan had been David's friend, minister, and counselor for years. He had encouraged David in his grand project to build a temple to Jehovah. Then he was sent to tell him that because he had been a man of war, another, his son, should build the temple. As the successor to Samuel, Nathan had seen David increase in power and splendor and had rejoiced at the favor bestowed upon him by God. But now he must go to him and rebuke him for his sin. I am sure Nathan prayed long and wept much before he preached that sermon to David.

With heavy feet and anxious heart Nathan ascended the steps to the palace where he had gone so often before. Had he commenced with a strong denunciation of David for his triple crime of adultery, hypocrisy, and murder, it probably would have aroused the anger of David instead of working repentance in his heart. But wise Nathan took another course. He knew that David was naturally a just, kind, magnanimous man. Nathan appealed to that sense of right and justice. He appealed to the better man in David. All preachers would do well to study the method of Nathan and learn how to touch the hidden springs of penitence and remorse.

To accomplish his purpose, Nathan told David the story of two men, one rich, the other poor—so poor that all he had was one little ewe lamb. This little lamb, as the traveler in the Near East today will often see it, was a family pet. It played with the man's children, slept in his bosom at night, and drank out of his own cup. One day there came a traveler to visit the rich man. Instead of taking of his own numerous flock, the rich man, despite the protests of the owner and the piteous pleas of the children, seized the poor man's lamb and dressed it for his guest.

The parable had the effect upon David that Nathan was sure it would have. It awakened his better nature; it roused his sense of justice. You can see his eye flash and his hand reach for the hilt of his sword, as he exclaimed, "As the Lord liveth, the man that hath done this thing shall surely die: and he shall restore the lamb fourfold" (2 Sam. 12:5–6).

So intent had David been upon Nathan's moving tale, that he never thought it could have reference to his own sin. Yet when he said, "The man that hath done this thing shall surely die," David passed sentence upon himself. Then Nathan drove the point of the sword into David's heart—"Thou art the man!" (v. 7).

Now watch David as Nathan showed him why he was "the man." He reminded him how God had delivered him out of the hand of Saul and anointed him king over Israel; how he had strengthened his kingdom and blessed him with power and prosperity. But David had shown his gratitude by a cruel and dastardly crime. "Wherefore hast thou despised the commandment of the Lord, to do evil in his sight? thou hast killed Uriah the Hittite with the sword, and hast taken his wife to be thy wife, and hast slain him with the sword of the children of Ammon. Now therefore the sword shall never depart from thine house; because thou hast despised me, and hast taken the wife of Uriah the Hittite to be thy wife. . . . . Behold, I will raise up evil against thee out of thine own house. . . . Thou didst it secretly: but I will do this thing before all Israel, and before the sun" (vv. 9–12).

Never was so tender, but so severe, a sermon ever preached. And what did David do? Had he done as other oriental kings would have done, Nathan's head would have rolled in the dust. But David bowed his head and said to Nathan, "I have sinned against the LORD" (v. 13a). But what about Uriah? Yes, he had wronged Uriah, but his sin was against God. As he put it in his penitential psalm, "Against thee, thee only, have I sinned, and done this evil in thy sight" (Ps. 51:4). Augustine, asked once how David could say that when he had so cruelly wronged Uriah, answered, "Because God only is without sin."

When David confessed his sin, the promise of forgiveness was immediate: "The LORD . . . hath put away thy sin" (2 Sam. 12:13b). The coming of a soul to true repentance may be a long and slow process, but the forgiveness of God never tarries. David's thirty-second psalm records this immediate forgiveness: "I said, I will confess my transgressions unto the LORD; and thou forgavest the iniquity of my sin" (Ps. 32:5). The storm has passed, and the rainbow of mercy spans the heavens. Now angels of heaven, some of whom have not struck a note on your harps since David fell, once again take up your harps and, sweeping all the chords, sing that sweetest of all songs—the song of the angels rejoicing over one sinner that repents!

But Nathan's sermon was not finished. He pronounced full forgiveness for the king. But he also told him that because his sin had made—and still makes—the enemies of God to blaspheme, the sword of temporal calamity would never depart from his house. It never did. In his wrath against the man of Nathan's tale who slaughtered the poor man's lamb, David said, quoting the law of Moses, "He shall restore fourfold." How fourfold was the retribution that fell upon David! See what happened to his four sons. The youngest, the child just born to Bathsheba who, although he lived so short a time, had wound his little life around his father's heart, was smitten and died. Another son, Amnon, who had defiled his sister, Tamar, was slain by Absalom. A third son, Absalom, drove his father from the throne and then was slain in the battle in the wood of

Ephraim with brokenhearted David, remembering his own transgressions, lamenting over him as he ascended to the chamber
over the gate: "O my son Absalom, my son, my son Absalom!
would God I had died for thee, O Absalom, my son, my son!"
(2 Sam. 18:33). And the fourth son, Adonijah, filled his father's
dying chamber with the noise of rebellion as he tried to seize
the throne and was slain by the fifth son, Solomon.

Yes, David's sin made the enemies of God to blaspheme, and
David had to pay. But the sin of David has never made the friends
of God to blaspheme. No, it has made the friends of God to
sorrow. It has made them be on their guard, not merely against
this one kind of sin but against other sins and all sins. It has
made them say, "If this could happen to the man after God's
heart, the man who wrote the twenty-third psalm and the ninety-
first psalm, then what might not happen to me?" It has shown
them how sin deceives, blinds, hardens, enslaves. It has made
the friends of God say, "Who can understand his errors?" (Ps.
19:12). It has made them confess that "the heart is deceitful above
all things, and desperately wicked" (Jer. 17:9). It has made them
say, "Search me, O God, and know my heart: try me, and know
my thoughts: and see if there be any wicked way in me, and lead
me in the way everlasting" (Ps. 139:23–24).

The Opened Windows

George H. Morrison (1866–1928) assisted the great Alexander Whyte in Edinburgh, pastored two churches, and then, in 1902, became pastor of the distinguished Wellington Church on University Avenue in Glasgow, Scotland. His preaching drew great crowds; in fact, people had to line up an hour before the services to ensure that they got seats in the large auditorium. Morrison was a master of imagination in preaching, yet his messages are solidly biblical.

From his many published volumes of sermons, I have chosen this message found in *Sunrise: Addresses from a City Pulpit*, published in 1903 by Hodder and Stoughton, London.

GEORGE H. MORRISON

9

The Opened Windows

His windows being open in his chamber toward Jerusalem.
(Daniel 6:10)

IT WAS IN AN HOUR of very sore distress that Daniel acted in the manner of which our text speaks. The crisis had come that he had long expected, and the crisis drove him to the feet of God. In the years that immediately preceded the Scottish Reformation, there was one thing that rankled in the breast of all true Scotsmen. It was the presence and the power of Frenchmen in almost all the high offices of state in Scotland. In much the same way there was widespread irritation, rising at times into very bitter envy, among the aristocratic patriots of Babylon at the powerful eminence of foreigners like Daniel. In Scotland, David Rizzio was assassinated, but Babylon was more advanced in civilization than Scotland. The presidents and the princes and the counselors took a more politic way of accomplishing their designs. Men were forbidden to pray for thirty days. They must ask no petition of any God or man, save of Darius. And it was then, when the royal decree was signed, and when Daniel fully recognized his peril, that he went into his house to pray, his windows being open toward Jerusalem.

So much for the historical setting of the words. Now, bringing

119

them into a larger environment, I find that they carry three
suggestions. The first is the moral significance of indifferent
actions. The second is the true relationship of the unseen and
the seen. The third is the right attitude toward the unattainable. Allow me to dwell on each for a few moments.

The Moral Significance of Indifferent Actions

First, then, whenever I think of Daniel's procedure, it reminds me of the moral significance of indifferent actions. There
was nothing remarkable in opening a window; it is one of those
common acts which we do without a thought. The Babylonian
slaves in Daniel's house would not attach the slightest importance to it. Yet, every time that Daniel opened that lattice, it
spoke of a heart that was traveling to Jerusalem. It was the index of a soul that in seductive Babylon was true to the God
and the temple of its race. It revealed a spirit that honors could
not destroy, a love that distance was powerless to quench, a
heroism that no impending doom could shake. The action in
itself was immaterial, but we see how full of significance it was.

There is another verse in the Old Testament that I should
like you to note in connection with our text. I read in Genesis
that when Abram and Lot parted, Lot "pitched his tent toward
Sodom" (13:12). There was no fault to be found with the actual place of pitching. It was just like a hundred other scenes
of bivouac. There was good pasture for the weary flocks, a brook
to wash off the soiling of the day, and sufficient shelter from
the keen night winds. Viewed in itself, the choice was immaterial. It was like the opening and closing of a lattice. The moral
significance lies in the word *toward*—Lot pitched his tent that
night toward Sodom. It was the direction, not the place, that
was important. It was the trend of the journey, not the actual
pitch. Had Lot been traveling away from Sodom, the site would
presumably have been ideal. But Daniel opened his windows
toward Jerusalem, and so doing revealed a heart true to the
highest. Lot pitched his tent toward Sodom, and ˙he tragedy
lay in the direction.

The truth, then, that I wish to impress on you is this: that there are actions which are quite indifferent in themselves and which in themselves, when viewed in isolation, may have no moral importance whatsoever. Yet if they reveal the trend of character, and the direction that our thoughts and wishes and feelings are setting in, no man dare say that they are immaterial. It is not the actual achievement of my life, it is my life's direction that is of supreme importance. As the handful of grass thrown up into the wind will tell where the wind comes and where it is going, and as the straw will show which way the current runs, so deeds, intrinsically insignificant, may be big with meaning if they disclose the movement of a life.

There are some things that are always and everywhere right. There are other things that in all circumstances are wrong. It is impossible to conceive a state of being, for instance, in which falsehood should be a virtue or bravery a vice. But in between these everlasting fixities, there lies a whole world of endeavor and of action, and the moral value of the action is determined by the trend and purpose of the underlying character. A score of lattices might be flung wide in Babylon, and might indicate nothing save that the heat was lessening. But the lattice of Daniel, open toward Jerusalem, was the witness of an heroic heart. And a score of tents might be pitched in the plains where Lot was and might mean no more than that the pasturage was good. But the tent of Lot, pitched there toward Sodom, told of a character hurrying to ruin.

I read the other day a characteristic anecdote about Professor Faraday. The lecture was over, and he was leaving the classroom when some little article dropped from his hand on the floor. The professor searched for it, but it was nowhere to be found. It is extraordinary how things will hide themselves on a level floor. And one of his students who was with him said, "Never mind, sir, it is of no consequence whether we find it tonight or no." "That is quite true," said the professor, "but it is of the gravest consequence to me that I be not baffled in my determination to find it." He knew the moral value of such actions. We are all too ready to say, "It does not matter." We are too fond of thinking, "What's the harm?" We isolate our actions, view them abstractly, judge them by inexorable codes of right and wrong. But the man who is in earnest about moral excellence will never forget the complexity of character. He will feel that what for other men is harmless, for him may be a step toward degradation. The supreme question is where is he tending—is it toward Sodom or is it toward Jerusalem?

The True Relationship of the Unseen and the Seen

In the second place, I catch a glimpse in our text of the true relationship of the unseen and the seen.

When Daniel opened his window, as was his custom, it was not Babylon that he desired to see. His heart was far away in his own country. Just as the Scottish emigrant in Canada dreams of the mountains and moors where he was born, of the glen and the burn swollen with the rain, and of the dripping bracken and the glory of purple heather, so Daniel in exile, heartsick if not homesick, craved for the land and the temple that he loved. He could not see them; they were beyond his vision. It would bring them no nearer to fling wide the lattice. Yet an instinct that every one of us can understand moved him to open the window toward Jerusalem. He could brook no barrier between him and the unseen.

And then, what happened when the window was opened? Why, the life in Babylon broke in on Daniel noisily. It had been dulled and deadened and indistinct before, but now it rolled like a tide into the room. He heard the wagon laboring through the street and the wagoners shouting in their upland dialect. He heard the angry chaffering in the market and the voices of children romping in the squares. He saw the aged resting in the shadow and the mothers with their infants in their arms. And now a soldier, now a laden country-woman, now a beggar, and now a Chaldean priest passed by under the open lattice. It was not to see all this that Daniel opened his window. His window was open to the unseen Jerusalem. But in the very instant of his opening it so, the life around him became doubly real.

Now that is like a little parable of something that happens to the truly religious man. Let him open the window of his heart on the unseen and the life at his door grows doubly real to him. It is not true that a heart-hunger for the unseen robs the life around us of its charm and import. The surging and strange life of common streets, the crooning of motherhood, and the song of children are touched into meanings hitherto undreamed of when the lattice of the soul is opened Christward. When the gaze of the heart is toward its unseen Savior, then do we love because He first loved us. And slowly but surely, kindled by love's insight, there grows the vision of the worth of life. We cannot despise men for whom Jesus lived. We cannot scorn men for whom Jesus died. We cannot be indifferent to human suffering, when we remember the compassion of the Savior. We cannot think lightly of motherhood or childhood when we recall the home at Nazareth. The life in the street, so colored and so changeful; the life in the cottage, with its joy and pain; childhood and age; and suffering and sorrow—all are enriched and illumined and transfigured when the soul's window is opened toward Jerusalem.

There is no such instance in history of this as the life of Jesus Christ Himself. He is the peerless example of that true relationship that is suggested to us by the text. He lived and moved among eternal things. He enjoyed unbroken fellowship with God. His heart was in heaven where His Father dwelled as truly as the heart of Daniel was in Jerusalem. Yet, though all the windows of His soul were opened heavenward, the life around Him was infinitely precious. The meanest villager ceased to be insignificant to a heart whose lattice was thrown wide on God. He could not disown the woman at the well; He dare not spurn the woman who was a sinner. He was moved with compassion for the widow of Nain, and he wept before the grave of Lazarus. There was never an anger like the anger of Jesus; there was never a pity so resourceful and so strong. No man could charge

our Lord with other-worldliness. His vision of God was no ecstatic rapture. All things around Him were more real and near
because the window was open toward Jerusalem.

The Right Attitude Toward the Unattainable

Lastly, and very briefly, our text suggests the right attitude
toward the unattainable. Daniel had thriven very well in exile
and had risen to quite remarkable power. But chains are still
chains however they be gilded, and Daniel was a prisoner in
Babylon. He would never again cross the fords of Jordan nor
ever look upon the Holy City. His prospects of return were
hopeless, and he was doomed to a perpetual separation. Yet,
though all hope of seeing Jerusalem was banished, we read that
he opened his windows toward Jerusalem and that suggests to
me the right attitude toward the unattainable.

For every man who is striving to live nobly is struggling after things he cannot reach. He has his Jerusalem, but it is far
away, and he knows that on this side of the grave he will not
see it. Dimly, and as in the mystical distance, he has grown
conscious of an ideal character. But the failure and the flaw of
every day, the recurrent weakness, and the unbridled heart tell
him too plainly that he is far off from it. It is when we feel that
deeply that we are tempted to despair. It is in such hours that
we fall to lower levels. We grow heartsick that we shall never
see Jerusalem. Let us be contented with our little room.

But, I say to you, dare to be a Daniel. Fling wide the lattice
toward what you can never reach. Have the casement open toward the unattainable, and by the open casement be in prayer.
And though the love and purity you long for, and all the depth
and strength of perfect character be as far distant from your
hungry heart as Judea from the yearning heart of Daniel, yet
in the very craving lies nobility and the pledge of attainment
in the tearless morn. Daniel today—in the sunshine and love of
God, in the land where they fear no death and need no temple—
possesses and enjoys all that he craved for once when he opened
his windows toward Jerusalem.

Preparation for Service

George Campbell Morgan (1863–1945) was the son of a British Baptist preacher and preached his first sermon when he was thirteen years old. He had no formal training for the ministry, but his tireless devotion to the study of the Bible helped him to become one of the leading Bible teachers of his day. Rejected by the Methodists, he was ordained into the Congregational ministry. He was associated with Dwight L. Moody in the Northfield Bible conferences and was an itinerant Bible teacher. He is best known as the pastor of the Westminster Chapel, London (1904–1917 and 1933–1943). During his second term there, he had Dr. D. Martyn Lloyd-Jones as his associate.

Morgan published more than sixty books and booklets, and his sermons are found in *The Westminster Pulpit* (London: Hodder and Stoughton, 1906–1916). This sermon was taken from volume 2.

GEORGE CAMPBELL MORGAN

10

Preparation for Service

In the year that king Uzziah died I saw the Lord sitting upon a
throne, high and lifted up; and his train filled the temple. Above
him stood the seraphim: each one had six wings; with twain he
covered his face, and with twain he covered his feet, and with
twain he did fly. And one cried unto another, and said, Holy, holy,
holy, is Jehovah of hosts: the whole earth is full of his glory. And
the foundations of the thresholds shook at the voice of him that
cried, and the house was filled with smoke. Then said I, Woe is
me! for I am undone; because I am a man of unclean lips, and I
dwell in the midst of a people of unclean lips: for mine eyes have
seen the King, Jehovah of hosts. Then flew one of the seraphim
unto me, having a live coal in his hand, which he had taken with
the tongs from off the altar: and he touched my mouth with it,
and said, Lo, this hath touched thy lips; and thine iniquity is taken
away, and thy sin forgiven. And I heard the voice of the Lord,
saying, Whom shall I send, and who will go for us? Then I said,
Here am I; send me. And he said, Go. (Isaiah 6:1–9 ASV)

STANDING AS WE do on the threshold of our winter's work, feeling
that we are coming to days of harvest and of gracious
ingathering, the question of my own heart has been, Lord, what
have You to say to me? I feel that if I can but hear what He has
to say to me, I may venture to pass the word on to you.

This passage of Scripture is familiar to us all. In the middle of the ninth verse the revelation of perpetual principles ends. After that we have the commission spoken to Isaiah concerning his own time. He was commissioned to utter a message of devastating judgment. We are not commissioned to utter that message. The local and the incidental occupy the last half of this chapter. The essential and the eternal occupy the first part.

The opening words of this passage fix in the history of the Hebrew people the event it recounts. "In the year that king Uzziah died." The reign of Uzziah over Judah, which lasted for fifty-two years, was over, and his son Jotham was about to succeed to the throne. Israel was suffering under the fearful tyranny of a military despotism. Shallum came to the throne by the murder of his predecessor. Menahem came to the throne by the murder of Shallum. Pekahiah succeeded his father but was murdered by Pekah. And now Pekah was on the throne, reigning over a people who were soon to be scattered.

The reign of Uzziah had been remarkable in many respects. When he ascended the throne fifty-two years before, as a youth if sixteen, he had set himself to seek God and the issue had been a period of remarkable prosperity. He had conducted a series of victorious campaigns against the enemies of God, by which he restored much lost territory. Following these, he brought about internal development—the building of towers, the making of cisterns, the planting of the land and its cultivation, and the increasing of husbandry. It was a wonderful reign to a certain point. Then his heart became lifted up, and the man who was victorious over the perils of adversity was overcome by the perils of prosperity. He rebelled against God and was smitten with leprosy, and for the last period of his life lived in a lazar house. At last he died.

It was at this point that there came to Isaiah, the son of Amoz, the vision recounted in this chapter. He had lived in Judah and had known no occupant of the throne of his own people other than the king who had now passed away. In the economy of God the time had now arrived when he should come forth to his definite and public ministry. In this wonderful passage we have the story of his solemn ordination.

The passage falls into two parts: the vision and the voice.

In the first verse these are the outstanding words: "I saw the Lord." In verse five we have the answer to that: "Then said I, Woe is me!" In verse eight we have the outstanding words of the second division: "I heard the voice of the Lord." In the last part of the same verse is the answer: "Then I said, Here am I; send me."

Take the simplest of these sentences that we may have the outline of the study on our minds: "I saw the Lord"; "Then said I"; "I heard the voice of the Lord"; and "Then I said." A vision and a voice, and in that order. First, the vision with all that it meant of revelation to the soul of this man of truth concerning God and, consequently, of truth concerning himself and all that it led onto of cleansing. And then, and not until then, the voice, "Whom shall I send, and who will go for us?" First the vision and then the voice. First the personal relationship to essential Light and Love and then the relative commission in obedience to which the man illuminated and cleansed went out to do the work of God. If I am to do anything for my Master, today, tomorrow, and the next day, I must have this vision, I must hear this voice. My answer to the vision must be Isaiah's answer, and my answer to the voice must be his also.

The Vision

Let us, then, first examine the vision. What did Isaiah see? The first thing that is impressed upon the mind in the study of the passage is that the prophet saw an occupied throne. "I saw the Lord sitting upon a throne, high and lifted up; and his train filled the temple." That is the first truth that broke upon the soul of the prophet with such terrific force and power that he spoke as though he had never seen the vision before. As a matter of fact, this man had long seen the Lord high and lifted up, but the empty throne was the occasion that revealed to him the true significance of the filled throne.

"In the year that King Uzziah died." The news spread from
street to street, from town to town, from village to village, that
the king was dead. There came to Isaiah the sense of loss in the
passing of the king. Chaos was everywhere. Israel was in such a
terrible condition that she could not exist any longer nationally.
Judah was following hard and fast in the wake of Israel to the
same defeat and disaster. The one throne to which Isaiah had
looked for support was empty. Men said to the psalmist, "If the
foundations be destroyed, what can the righteous do?" (Ps. 11:3).

And that, perchance, was the first feeling that came to the
heart of the prophet when the throne of Judah was empty. Who
now will succeed? Then, "In the year that king Uzziah died I
saw the Lord sitting upon a throne." Behind the empty throne,
there is a throne that is never empty. Over the chaos that ap-
palls the heart, there is the God of order and government.

I think if we had cross-examined Isaiah, he would have been
unable to describe the personality upon which his eyes rested,
but he saw the Lord. A person was manifested to him. Through
this whole book of Isaiah is presented a personality vague and
undefined; a personality that startles us with contradictions; a
personality robed in splendor, girded with strength, with government sitting upon His shoulders; a personality stripped,
wounded, bruised, suffering; a King reigning in righteousness
and prosecuting His propaganda to the end of the ages; and
through all the spheres, a bruised and broken Man who says,
"Who hath believed our report? and to whom hath the arm of
the Lord been revealed?" (John 12:38). Vague shadowy out-
lines, never quite clear until the New Testament is in your hand,
but nevertheless a person. Isaiah's first vision of this person
was so vague that he could not perfectly describe it, so definite that he said, "I saw the Lord."

He proceeded immediately from the description of the central person to that of the surrounding facts—seraphim, flaming glory, smoke, reverberating thunder, and the maintenance
of a song—but the person is mentioned and left, "I saw the
Lord." The essential truth is that of a person enthroned.

There is a very beautiful connection between the twelfth chapter of the gospel of John and the whole prophecy of Isaiah. It is the chapter of Jesus overshadowed by the Cross. The first incident is that of Mary's coming very near to His grief and breaking the alabaster box of ointment upon His feet. The second incident is that of His entrance to Jerusalem, which we call the Triumphal Entry, all full of sorrow to Him. The third incident is that of the coming of the Greeks. The Cross is everywhere. It was the shadow of the Cross that drew forth the adoring worship of Mary, that filled His own eyes with tears as He rode into Jerusalem, that made Him reply when Greeks asked to see Him, "Except a grain of wheat fall into the earth and die, it abideth by itself alone" (v. 24).

Now look at verse forty-one in this chapter: "These things said Isaiah, because he saw his glory" (v. 41). What said Isaiah? "Lord, who hath believed our report?" "These things said Isaiah, because he saw his glory." Isaiah's conception in chapter fifty-three of the mystery and the agony of rejection had been made tremendous because he saw His glory. When did he see His glory? When he was commissioned for His work. "I saw the Lord sitting upon a throne, high and lifted up." The first thing the prophet saw before he went forth to work that was to be hard and perilous and difficult was the vision of the enthroned God. The throne of Judah is empty. There is chaos everywhere. For this man the throne is filled, and out of the chaos the cosmos is coming.

He next proceeded to speak of the surrounding glory, the seraphim, the flames of fire, the hosts of the Most High God, six-winged seraphim. In the presence of that personality, with two wings they veiled their faces, with two they veiled their feet, with two they were perpetually flying. This is, of course, symbolic, and we can interpret such symbolism only by Eastern thought. The face is the symbol of intellectual apprehension, the feet are the symbols of governmental procedure, the wings are symbolic of activity divinely inspired. The unveiling of the nature of the enthroned One is seen in the activity of the burning spirits that surround the throne. They veil their faces, unable to come to perfect intellectual apprehension of the mystery of His being. They veil their feet, for while they are principalities, do-minions, rulers, their governmental procedure gains its strength from submission to His throne. The veiling of the feet is the hiding of personal authority in the presence of supreme author-ity. But the wings, the remaining wings, are ever active, inspired by the very Spirit of life. They perpetually serve under the au-thority of His throne.

Now listen to the song. It is a twofold song. First, the song of the nature of the enthroned One. "Holy, holy, holy, is Jehovah of hosts" (Isa. 6:3). Then it is a song about earth. I am always so thankful when I come to this. It is a song about earth in that high presence chamber with the enthroned Jehovah revealed personally, but so that He cannot be described, surrounded by the flaming spirits that veil their faces of intelligence, and their feet of government, and beat their wings in perpetual service. What is this they sing of the earth? "The whole earth is full of his glory," or notice the marginal reading of the revised version, "the fulness of the whole earth is his glory." These spirits that surround the throne look down to the earth and see God's glory in it. Isaiah has a different vision of it pres-ently. These spirits saw his vision also, but they are singing in the presence of God of an ultimate triumph of truth, a final restoration, a final victory. They are singing by faith and hope in the presence of God of the victory that is to be. "The whole earth is full of his glory." The great psalm of the King, which describes His procedure to ultimate victory, ends with the words that the seraphim sang in the presence of God. "The whole earth is full of his glory." So that the psalm of the glory of God, which is part of the inheritance of the saint here and now amid the chaos and the darkness and the strife and the battle, is the perpetual song that angels sing.

Notice for a moment the effect of the song on the earthly temple. The very "thresholds were moved"–trembled. "The house was filled with smoke." We shall be perfectly correct if we translate this word "smoke" by the word "anger." In Psalm 80:4, we read, "O Jehovah, God of hosts, how long wilt thou be angry against the prayer of thy people?" The literal translation of this is, "How long wilt thou smoke against the prayer of thy people?" The connection shows that smoke is a symbol of anger. In the day of God's activity it is said by the ancient prophet Joel that there shall be "blood, and fire, and pillars of smoke" (2:30). Isaiah, in that high presence chamber, saw the uplifted God upon His throne, and saw the burning spirits around the throne veiling their faces and feet and ceaselessly moving to do His bidding. He heard their song, the song of ultimate victory, in the earth itself, and yet there was the trembling of things in the temple of God. There was the filling of the house with smoke, typical of His anger. So this man stood in the midst of the awful vision, conscious of God's holiness, and His enthronement, conscious of the victory that must be final, and yet conscious that anger was abroad, that judgment was out on the highway of the Most High. The house trembled and was filled with smoke.

And now how did he answer the vision? The answer was not a prepared one. The greatest words men speak in the presence of God, either about God or to God, are words that come surging out of the deepest consciousness, words that must be spoken because no others are fit. And when this man stood in the midst of the glory, when for a moment his eyes were unveiled, what did he say? Oh, the agony of the cry, "Woe is me! for I am undone; because I am a man of unclean lips, and I dwell in the midst of a people of unclean lips." All of which means that when the prophet had a clear vision of God, he had the true vision of man. And when the prophet had the clearer vision of the divine order, he had a more overwhelming sense of human disaster. Notice that the cry concerning himself proceeds backward, from effect to cause. The effect, "Woe is me!" The reason of the woe, "I am undone." The reason of the being undone, "I am a man of unclean lips."

Why unclean lips only? Why did he not say unclean heart?

Why did he not say unclean spirit? Again, the language is symbolic, and it is most simple symbolism. Let us look at the epistle of James: "The tongue is a fire: the world of iniquity among our members is the tongue, which defileth the whole body, and setteth on fire the wheel of nature, and is set on fire by hell. For every kind of beasts and birds, of creeping things and things in the sea, is tamed, and hath been tamed by mankind. But the tongue can no man tame; it is a restless evil, it is full of deadly poison" (3:6–8). As in the divine the Word is the expression of the God, so in the human the speech of man is the expression of man and the lips and the tongue are the instruments of speech.

This man standing in the presence of the glory confesses that his lips are polluted. Let Jesus speak: "The things which proceed out of the mouth come forth out of the heart; and they defile the man" (Matt. 15:18). Within is the fountain head of corruption, but it is poured out and expressed through the tongue and the lips, and so Isaiah says, "I am undone; because I am a man of unclean lips." The words are unclean because the fact that they have to express is an unclean fact. What has this to do with his work? Everything. I do not know how you all feel, but the most stupendous evidence to my heart, every day growing, of the grace of God is not that He saves me. That is a great evidence of grace, amazing grace! But the most stupendous evidence of God's grace is that when He saves me He consents to use me. And one of the first qualifications for being ready is to have stood in the presence of His glory and to have found out how unworthy I am to utter His message. God almighty is my witness that I am not speaking to you idly. Every day I am more astonished that God should use me at all.

And what follows? I do not know that it would not be good to sit still and read the rest almost without comment. It is so simple. "Then"—I wish I knew how to emphasize that "then," because it is the dividing line. We have tried to look at the glory of God, at the enthroned Jehovah, at this man smitten in his inner consciousness with a sense of unworthiness. Then what?

"Then flew one of the seraphim." Taking in his hand one of the sacred vessels from the altar, the place of blood and fire, and catching one of the burning coals from the altar, he comes to that man.

Now, whereas I want to speak especially of the fact that for the man called to service there is perfect cleansing and energizing provided, what I want you to see first is that out of the midst of the overwhelming and awful glory of God comes the most overwhelming vision of His grace: the enthroned Jehovah surrounded by the burning spirits that worship. Do you hear the thunder of the seraphim as they sing? Can you hear anything else? I do not think I can. God can! What did He hear? The cry of a guilty man! Oh, soul of mine, take heart. One guilty man cries out in the consciousness of his sin, and the faint cry of that human soul, conscious of pollution, rises in the ear of God above the thunder of the seraphim. And a seraph must leave the place of worship to work when a human soul is in need. These are divine measurements. These are not the measures we sometimes put upon evangelistic effort. That was evangelistic effort. And he brought the live coal and he touched the lips of the man, he touched that which the man had made the symbol of his own uncleanness. The man said, "I am undone; because I am a man of unclean lips," and the seraph touched the lips, and said, "Lo, this hath touched thy lips; and thine iniquity is taken away, and thy sin forgiven."

This is one of the cases where I am almost inclined to translate iniquity very literally as to the actual meaning of the word: "Thy crookedness has been taken away." Fire has straightened you out! But something more: "Thy sin is forgiven." Sin is offense, guilt, the thing in a man that is the outcome of his iniquity in his relation to God. What of that? It is forgiven, and here you may use the old Hebrew word, "thy sin is expiated." It is the word that the Hebrew made use of when he referred to atonement. It is the word to cover over, not in the sense of covering over a polluted thing, but to atone, to blot out. Your sin, as against this high excellence and glory of heaven, is expiated.

Thy personal crookedness is straightened out. Your relative guilt is expiated.

And how was it done? By the coal of fire from the altar, and God Almighty cannot deal with Isaiah in his uncleanness except by the coal of fire that comes from the altar.

The Voice

What follows? Perhaps a pause. I do not know. There is no pause in the letterpress. I think there must have been a pause, a waiting moment, in which this man rose into the great consciousness that he was undone no longer, that his lips were no longer impure but purified. It is as he waited in that great consciousness that the voice came. He had seen the vision of God. This was the outcome. Now the voice and how much it says: "Whom shall I send, and who will go for us?" Who will go? God is asking for volunteers. God needs someone to be sent, someone who will go. What is the question? Who is ready to be sent? "Whom shall I send?" "Who will go for us?" And the emphasis in that second question is not on the "Go," but on "for us." Who will be ready when I send them? Who will be in readiness to be sent, ready to represent us? And then, thank God, notwithstanding that this man but a moment ago had expressed his consciousness of pollution, immediately came the answer: "Here am I; send me." "Here am I," that is abandonment; "send me," that is readiness. He could not have said that until his lips had been touched by the coal from the altar. The vision cursed him, but the fire cleansed him; and now when God wants help, this cleansed man says, I am at Your disposal.

That is the whole law of service. To do successful service, I need first a vision of God enthroned. Have you this vision of God? If you are not quite sure whether God's throne is tottering, you had better retire. You remember God's method of sifting an army. It was a wonderful method. Thirty-two thousand came out and said, "We are all ready." And the first test was, "Let the men fearful and afraid go home." And twenty-two thousand men turned right about face and marched home.

Are you sure that was not a mistake? No, for in the day of battle
the man who has fear in his heart is a peril. When the victory
was won, they all came back to shout. God bless them! But when
we are fighting we do not want them.

Can we see God on His throne? That is the question. We
can see the chaos. We are very blind if we cannot—national
corruption, municipal rottenness, dilettante fooling with the
problems of poverty that ought to be the problem of every
statesman. But high over all earthly thrones is the throne that
never trembles. If you can see God on His throne, then that
throne is commissioning you to take the evangel of the crucified Christ to cure all the ills of humanity. That is our message. We must have a vision of His enthronement, of His
holiness, and we must have this also—the vision of His ultimate
glory in the earth. And then we need the vision of self. If I
may have a vision of His glory, I need the true vision of self.
We need also the cleansing that He provides. We are not fit
for all this. But to stay there is to dishonor God. Remember:
the altar is there, and the fire is there. God help us to get to
the altar. He will cleanse us and purge us, and with a baptism
of fire make us all He wants us to be, if only we will let Him.
Let us look up into His face, solemnly and earnestly saying,
"By the vision of Your enthronement, by the matchless mercy
of the altar and the fire, here am I; send me."

Jeremiah: The Lure of the Wilderness

Clovis Gillham Chappell (1882–1972) was one of American Methodism's best-known and most effective preachers. He pastored churches in Washington, D.C.; Dallas and Houston, Texas; Memphis, Tennessee; and Birmingham, Alabama; and his pulpit ministry drew great crowds. He was especially known for his biographical sermons that made biblical figures live and speak to our modern day. He published about thirty volumes of sermons.

This message was taken from *Sermons on Old Testament Characters*, published in New York by Richard R. Smith, Inc., in 1930.

— 11 —

Jeremiah: The Lure of the Wilderness

O that I had in the wilderness a lodging place of wayfaring men; that I might leave my people, and go from them! for they be all adulterers, an assembly of treacherous men. (Jeremiah 9:2)

THIS LONGING TO LEAVE his people expressed by Jeremiah is altogether human. Jeremiah is not the only preacher who ever wanted to change his appointment. He is not the only worker who ever wanted to throw down his task and get away. Many of us have uttered this same cry. This is what the psalmist was saying long ago: "Oh that I had wings like a dove! for then would I fly away, and be at rest" (Ps. 55:6). There are some who begin to utter this longing in their very youth, and it grows more intense as they get deeper into the years and life becomes more serious with its baptisms of tears—tears over losses and tears over bitter disappointments.

Why Did Jeremiah Wish to Get Away?

He wished to escape an unpleasant task. He loved the country. But the wilderness lured him at present because it offered him a refuge from the tempestuous life of the city. God had called Jeremiah to be a prophet. In response to that call he had entered bravely upon his task. But he had not done so willingly. When Isaiah was called, he responded with eagerness: "Here am I; send me" (Isa. 6:8). His work seems a joy. He meets his conflicts with a noble zest. But not so Jeremiah. He protests and shrinks and begs to be excused. "Ah, Lord GOD! behold, I cannot speak: for I am a child" (Jer. 1:6).

But in spite of his shrinking and in spite of all protestations of his unfitness, the task is forced upon him. Therefore, he is now in the limelight, though the glare of it offends him. He is in the midst of turmoil and conflict, though he is a lover of peace and quiet. He is forced to fight and contend, though the whole business is hateful to him. "Woe is me, my mother, that thou hast borne me a man of strife and a man of contention to the whole earth!" (Jer. 15:10). He is traveling the prophet's road, but his feet bleed at every step that he takes. Therefore, it is only natural that he should want to leave his people and hike away to the wilderness.

Not only was the task of being a prophet distasteful to Jeremiah because of his peculiar temperament, but his natural dislike was greatly increased on account of the kind of congregation to which he had to preach. His work brought him into daily contact with men whose association was entirely disagreeable. He was a clean, high-souled, and sensitive idealist. Therefore, it was no little agony to be compelled to work constantly with men for whom he could find no more complimentary description than adulterers, traitors, slanderers, and forsakers of God. It is not a matter of wonder, therefore, that he should want to leave such an uncongenial congregation and flee into the wilderness.

It has never been my lot to serve but one church that was thoroughly disagreeable. This congregation was not so far gone as the congregation to which Jeremiah preached. But they were not altogether the type to win a pastor's heart. I recall with appreciation what my predecessor said to them in his farewell sermon. "This is," said he, "my last message. I wish to remark in closing that if everything is true about your former pastors that you have said about them, every one of them ought to be turned out of the church. If everything is true of you that you have told me about one another, the last one of you ought to be hanged. We will receive the benediction." And he departed with some of the joy that I think Jeremiah would have felt could he have escaped to that longed for lodging place for wayfaring men.

Then Jeremiah's task was made the more difficult and distasteful to him because his ministry had to be almost altogether a ministry of denunciation and of doom. He would have been delighted to say the pleasing thing and the complimentary thing. He would have been most glad to be a preacher of hope and a prophet of optimism. But his unrepentant and sinful people made it impossible. He was far too sincere to cry "Peace! peace!" when he knew there was no peace. He saw far too clearly to be blind to the fact that punishment must inevitably follow sin. While others were declaring that God would save His people under any circumstances, he was forced to declare that, unless they repented, they should be driven into exile. "What else can I do?" he has God asking. He knows that no nation can be "saved materially unless it is redeemed spiritually."

Jeremiah wanted to get away from persecution. The type of preaching that he was forced to do did not tend to make him popular. It did not win the applause and appreciation of his people. On the contrary, it made him exceedingly unpopular. It brought to him bitter opposition and persecution. At times that persecution took the form of cold neglect. When his sermon was over, folks did not come forward and congratulate him and tell him how they enjoyed it, as you tell your pastor. They chilled him by their neglect and froze him by their lack of sympathy. There is the sob of a sensitive and deeply wounded heart in the cry, "I sat alone because of thy hand" (Jer. 15:17). He was weighed down by the burden of a great loneliness.

But there were other times when the persecution he suffered took another form. Sometimes he was ridiculed. He complains that he is made a laughing stock all the day. And what a heavy burden that is! There are few things harder to bear than to have folks laugh at you, scorn you, pass you by in contempt as a mere fanatic. When his book of prophecies was put into the hands of the king, this pathetic substitute for royalty showed no slightest appreciation. On the contrary, he made plain his contempt for the old prophet by taking his penknife and cutting the roll to pieces and burning it in the fire.

Then there were times when yet sterner forms of persecution were used. One day he was stoned out of his native village as if he were a wild street dog. At other times, we find him suffering the pain and shame of the stocks. On another day, his back was bared to the smiters and he had to undergo the agony and humiliation of being publicly whipped. He became thoroughly acquainted with the inside of prisons. One time he comes before us with hands and feet stained with stenchful mud, for he has been starving at the bottom of an old well. And though he was rescued, this was not wrought by any friend of his. It was not the work of any member of his congregation. It was the work of a slave who was too humane to see the old man die by the inch. Therefore, we are not going to blame him if again and again he wished to leave his people and flee into the wilderness.

He wanted to leave because his ministry seemed an utter failure. No man, I think, ever preached with more passionate earnestness than did Jeremiah. He warned men night and day with tears. But his warnings were unheeded. His report was not believed. No man ever had a more fruitless ministry in his own day than did this prophet. It is hard enough to keep climbing when you are approaching nearer and nearer the summit. It is hard enough to keep fighting when victory is coming closer and closer. But to keep climbing when the summit seems to retreat from you and to keep fighting when victory becomes more and more remote, that is difficult indeed.

And remember that the pain of Jeremiah's failure was not the result of the sense of his own inability to win. The agony that he suffered over it was not born of the humiliation that it brought to him. His failure was inseparably connected with the failure of his people. His inability to reach them and to win them to repentance meant, so far as his own day was concerned, that his ministry had gone for nothing. But what was far harder to bear, it meant the loss and utter ruin of the people he loved. To stay by, therefore, meant not only the pain of toiling at a fruitless task, but the yet greater pain of watching the approaching death of the nation that he loved better than he loved his own life. His yearning to be permitted to leave has in it something of the shrinking agony of heartbroken Hagar as she cries, "Let me not see the death of [my] child!" (Gen. 21:16). He wanted to get away from a ministry whose failure meant not only his personal inability to win but also the yet more bitter heartache of watching his nation die.

Did Jeremiah Leave?

No, he did not. He was eager to go, yet he stayed. He yearned to run, yet he remained steadfast. He felt the lure of the wilderness, and yet he remained amid the turmoil and toil of the city. And this he did not because of any physical compulsion. He might have gone time and again, and his own people would have been glad to have him go. But in spite of the hatred of his people and his own shrinking from his task, he stood in his place and remained true for more than forty long, weary years.

Why Did Jeremiah Stay?

He remained steadfast from a sense of duty. The same bonds held him that held Paul. "Behold, I go bound in the spirit unto Jerusalem, not knowing the things that shall befall me there: save that the Holy Ghost witnesseth in every city, saying that bonds and afflictions abide me" (Acts 20:22–23). He stayed at his post because he felt that he ought to stay. When he uttered this cry, he knew that leaving for him was an impossibility. "Oh that I might leave." But what is implied is, "I cannot. I must stay."

"I must." That is a word that is frequently found in the vocabulary of moral giants. "Oh, that I might go," he said, "but I must stay. This I must do simply because it is my duty." Now there may not be so much of gush and of glow in a declaration of this kind as we would like. But surely you will agree that such a sense of duty is sorely needed today. Entirely too many of us let ourselves off with the doing of the easy or the pleasant. We listen for the voice of a shallow emotionalism. And failing to hear it, we give heed to the voice of laziness and indifference. We face the work we ought to do asking too often how we feel and too seldom what is our duty. Jeremiah listened to the voice of duty. Hence, he did the thing he ought to do regardless of whether he felt like it.

Jeremiah was bound to his post by the cords of a mighty conviction. He was absolutely sure of the truth of the message that God had given him to deliver. The fact that men refused to give heed did not in any sense lead him to doubt the truth of his message. There were times when it made it hard for him to preach. There were times when he even resolved to keep utter silence. But this resolution was soon shattered because the Word of God was as a burning fire shut up in his bones. Silence became unendurable. Under the pressure of an irresistible conviction, he felt himself compelled to speak. He was convinced, in spite of the fact that his message was being rejected, that its acceptance was his people's only hope.

There were many other prophets at that time, but their messages differed widely from the message of Jeremiah. They were prophets of an easy and sentimental optimism. They came with the popular cry of "Peace! peace!" upon their lips. But Jeremiah saw a different vision. He was as sure of God's love as the other prophets, but he did not forget the fact that as intensely as God loved His people, just so intensely did He hate their sin. He said with terrible clearness that if they did not repent, if they did not turn from their idolatry and adultery, God would be compelled to fling them out of His sight regardless of His love. He was gripped by the conviction that there was no safety for the individual nor for the nation without righteousness. Therefore, it is not to be wondered at that he remained to shriek his message into the ears of his people when he saw them hugging to themselves the damning delusion that God would save them even in their rebellion and in their mad clinging to their iniquities. This conviction that he had a message that offered his nation its one hope of salvation caused him to stand by his post when he fain would have fled to the restful and easeful life of the wilderness.

That same conviction should steady us. Is it a fact that we have all sinned and come short of the glory of God? Is it a fact that there is no other name under heaven given among men whereby we must be saved? Is it a fact that He is able to save to the uttermost them that come to God by Him? Do you know these facts? Do you accept them as facts? Then you must preach them. It is not a question of whether men applaud or hiss you. It is not a question of whether they throw mud at you or throw bouquets at you. We must speak the truth as God gives us to see it. To refuse is to spit in the face of conviction and throw away your crown.

Then Jeremiah was held to his task by the cords of love. These Jews had in them much that pained and grieved and disgusted and even angered this prophet. But in spite of all their sins, he loved them still. They were still his people. And though they fill him with indignation and though he declares he is full of the fury of the Lord against them, yet his heart is in their keeping and he cannot for the life of him turn away from them. Often his words scorch and blister and burn. Often his cheeks are flushed and his eyes are fiery with anger. Yet his heart is always full of love.

And do not think it strange that this prophet can be intensely angry and intensely loving at the same time. Love and anger are not in the least inconsistent. In fact, his anger was born of his love. If he had not loved, he would not have raged. If he had not loved, he would have gone complacently to the wilderness in perfect and broad-minded good humor. That is the secret of much that passes for tolerance today. It is merely utter indifference parading in the borrowed garments of tolerance.

Personally, I believe that it would be a distinct gain if some of us had more capacity for anger. Now I do not mean that particular type of anger that is the result of selfishness—that anger that you felt when you were not the principal speaker or did not get invited to the party. I mean the anger that comes to a morally sound man when right is trodden under the foot of might, when justice is made the victim of injustice. Jeremiah had a great capacity for anger. His words are hot and burning words to this day. No man ever rebuked more unsparingly, and the secret of it is that no man ever loved more tenderly. Therefore, though he shrieks at his congregation in white-heat anger, he stays with them until the very last because he is in the grip of a love that will not let him go.

Then Jeremiah remained at his post through the power of God. From what the Lord said to Jeremiah, it is evident that he was not by nature a staunch and courageous man. He was sensitive and timid and retiring. But God promised him in the very beginning that He would stand close for help. "Thou therefore gird up thy loins, and arise, and speak unto them all that I command thee: be not dismayed at their faces. . . . For, behold, I have made thee this day a defenced city, and an iron pillar, and brasen walls against the whole land . . . And they shall fight against thee; but they shall not prevail against thee; for I am with thee, saith the LORD, to deliver thee" (Jer. 1:17–19).

There is absolutely no accounting for the steadfastness of Jeremiah apart from this promise. As He in later years changed fluctuating Simon, the son of Jona, into a rock of Christlike character, so He turned Jeremiah into the opposite of what he was. This He did not independent of the prophet. He was able to do so because Jeremiah was a man constant and earnest in prayer. He opened the windows of his soul toward God, and the Spirit of the Almighty came in and made him strong. In all the Scriptures, I know of no finer example of the power of God to equip a man for the performance of a task that in the energy of the flesh was absolutely impossible. Surely this man learned long before St. Paul of the sufficiency of the grace of God.

What Was the Outcome?

So far as his own generation was concerned, Jeremiah lived and died almost an utter failure. When his nation was in ruins, the last handful of Jews that were left consulted him as to whether they should stay in their own land or flee into Egypt. He took the matter before the Lord and obtained an answer. He told them upon divine authority to remain in their own land. But, in spite of his warning, they fled into Egypt and carried the protesting and brokenhearted prophet with them. In Egypt, he spent his last tearful days, and he went on denouncing the sin of his wayward people. There he died, and there his ashes rest in a nameless grave. And his ministry continued a failure to the very end. Not one bit even of "sunset success" was granted to him.

But if he failed to be heard in his own generation, he has been heard by the subsequent centuries. His influence upon his own people has possibly been greater than that of any other of the prophets. But his influence has by no means been confined to his own nation. He has put his passionate hands upon all of the continents. We feel the uplift of his Spirit-filled personality as we meet in God's house today. And I dare to believe that as this redeemed saint looks back upon life from the midst of that innumerable company that have washed their robes and made them white in the blood of the Lamb, he sees of the travail of his soul and is satisfied.

A Study in Depression

John Daniel Jones (1865–1942) served for forty years at the Richmond Hill Congregational Church in Bournemouth, England, where he ministered the Word with a remarkable consistency of quality and effectiveness, as his many volumes of published sermons attest. A leader in his denomination, he gave himself to church extension (he helped to start thirty new churches), assistance to needier congregations, and increased salaries for the clergy. He spoke at D. L. Moody's Northfield Conference in 1919.

This sermon was taken from his book *The Hope of the Gospel,* published by Hodder and Stoughton in 1911.

12

A Study in Depression

And he [Elijah] requested for himself that he might die; and said,
It is enough; now, O LORD, take away my life; for I am not better
than my fathers. (1 Kings 19:4)

"ELIJAH," says the apostle James, "was a man of like passions with
us" (5:17 ASV); or, as the Twentieth Century Testament more
vividly expresses it, "Elijah was only a man like ourselves." "Only
a man like ourselves!" It is a startling and rather staggering
statements. For I imagine that what strikes most men in reading
Elijah's story is the *difference* between him and ourselves. He
was not the ordinary type of man at all. He was a man of
volcanic force. He was a man of granite strength. He was a
perfect Alp of a man. He was one of those men who emerge
occasionally in the world's history, who lift themselves far above
the common levels of humanity, and are made solitary and
lonely by their very size.

"Only a man like ourselves!"—that is almost the last remark
in the world I would think of making on the man who on
Carmel faced that mob of Baalitish priests and an apostate
nation. "Only a man like ourselves!" That is almost the last
remark in the world I would make about the man who, in virtue of some tremendous spiritual energy within, swept along

like a whirlwind and out distanced Ahab in his chariot in that wild race before the storm to Jezreel. "Only a man like ourselves!" That is almost the last remark in the world I would make about the man who confronted King Ahab at the entrance to Naboth's vineyard and pronounced doom upon him. This man of courage so splendid, of strength so magnificent, is an extraordinary man. He is almost a superhuman man. He strides among ordinary men like Gulliver amid the inhabitants of Lilliput.

But there is one event in the prophet's life that justifies the apostle's comment. When I see Elijah on Carmel, or at the entrance to Naboth's vineyard, I feel him to be in a class entirely by himself, a gigantic and abnormal man. But when I see him under the juniper tree, I realize that, after all, he was "only a man like ourselves." For it is not the man of superhuman strength I see here. I see a man as weak as water—tired, timid, discouraged, depressed, querulous, and fretful—whimpering out in his disappointment, "It is enough; now, O Lord, take away my life; for I am not better than my fathers." And when I see Elijah weak, depressed, and fretful, I know, in spite of Carmel and Naboth's vineyard, he was, after all, "only a man like ourselves."

Now at first, perhaps, this weakness strikes us as strange in a man of Elijah's build. All of a sudden Mr. Valiant-for-Truth seems to have changed places with Mr. Fearing. But, as a matter of fact, these alternations are common enough in actual life. There are ups and downs in the spiritual experiences of men. There are times when men, usually timid, become suddenly brave; there are times when men, usually brave, become suddenly timid. Mr. Fearing, for instance, so weak and timid at ordinary times, on one occasion at any rate, showed himself to be as brave as Greatheart or Steadfast or Valiant-for-Truth or any one of the company. "When he got into Vanity Fair," says John Bunyan, "he wanted to fight all the men of the fair." Indeed, this chickenhearted man, who could not face the perils of the way in his own strength, grew so hot against the fooleries of the fair and became so aggressively bold that he and Greatheart, his escort, were like both of them to be knocked on the head.

And if weak men sometimes suddenly become bold, bold and brave men sometimes suddenly become weak. Abraham was a bold and brave man. He ventured everything at the call of God. He went out not knowing where he went. It was enough for him that he was under God's guidance and in God's care. But Abraham lost faith and heart and hope and everything in Egypt. Mr. Valiant-for-Truth had become Mr. Fearing.

Peter was a bold and brave man—the Greatheart of the Twelve. When he said to his Master, "If I should die with thee, I will not deny thee in any wise" (Mark 14:31), he meant exactly what he said. He would cheerfully have faced death for the Lord that day. But Peter in the Judgment Hall was a panic-stricken liar and coward. His courage had all disappeared, and weakness and shameful fear had taken its place. Mr. Greatheart had become for the moment Mr. Fearing.

I suppose one of the strongest and bravest men who ever walked earth was Martin Luther. It needed a man of almost superhuman strength and courage to do the work he did. I think of him, for instance, riding to that Congress in Worms in face of the warnings and appeals of his friends, saying with a kind of frolicsome and reckless courage that he would go though there were as many devils in Worms as there were tiles upon the rooftops. He reminds me of the kind of courage this man Elijah showed when he faced the priests of Baal and an apostate people and a murderous king and queen on Carmel. But I follow Luther to the Wartburg, and in his friendly imprisonment there I find the erstwhile brave and fearless man full of nervousness and timidities, flinging his inkwell at imaginary devils, a prey to depression and weakness and fear. Mr. Greatheart, Mr. Valiant-for-Truth, had become Mr. Fearing.

And side by side with Martin Luther, as possessing that same kind of indomitable courage and strength, I might place John

Knox, the Scottish reformer. "He is not afraid," said some courtiers of him, as he came forth from one of his stormy interviews with Queen Mary. "Afraid?" said the reformer, who overheard the remark, "I have looked in the faces of many angry men, and yet have not been frightened above measure." That, indeed, was the testimony borne to him by the regent Morton as they laid his body in the churchyard of St. Giles: "There lies he who never feared the face of man." And yet I read of a day when the heart of the intrepid John Knox gave way, when his courage gave place to despair, and he cried, "I cannot win Scotland, let me die." Mr. Valiant-for-Truth had become Mr. Fearing.

And a similar alternation of feeling took place in Elijah. He was Mr. Valiant-for-Truth on Mount Carmel, alone against the world. He is Mr. Fearing when we see him beneath the juniper tree, weak and discouraged and praying that he might die. Alternations of feeling, therefore, such as we find here are by no means rare. Those who rise high often sink low. Strong, impulsive natures often fall into fits of depression. But these times of depression are usually explainable. They have their ascertainable causes. Elijah's depression and despair are explainable.

There were certain reasons for the weakness that is recorded here. I want, if I can, to find out what those reasons were. I want for a few minutes to inquire into the causes of Elijah's depression. The study may not be without its profit to us, for depression is not an unheard-of thing in these days of ours. We, too, get discouraged and despondent, and, like Elijah, are tempted to say that our work is of no use and to abandon it in weariness and despair. Now it is possible that the discovery of the reasons of Elijah's depression may throw some light upon the causes of the depression and discouragement from which we often suffer. To discover the causes of our malady is to be well on the way toward the discovery of the cure. Well, now, when I turn to the narrative, I find that one cau_ of Elijah's depression was his physical weariness.

Elijah's Physical Weariness

He had to betake himself to a hurried flight to escape the murderous wrath of the queen who had vowed to kill him within twenty-four hours, as the priests of Baal had been slain on Carmel. He had fled first of all to Beersheba and left his servant there. Then he had gone another day's journey into the wilderness. He was a worn-out, spirit-tired man when he flung himself down under the juniper tree.

Now everybody knows that mind and body interact and affect one another in the most intimate and vital way. To have an absolutely sound and healthy mind you must have an absolutely sound and healthy body. It is the recognition of this fact that supplies the substratum of truth there is in Christian Science and faith healing. I have no doubt that most of us could quote wonderful instances of the triumph of the spirit over the weakness of the flesh. But, speaking broadly, a man's spiritual condition is largely determined by the state of his physical health. There is no one here who does not know that when we are tired and spent the very grasshopper becomes a burden. Difficulties and little inconveniences that would not worry us at all, if we were fresh and strong, become almost more than we can bear when we are weary and worn. There is no need for me to amplify. We know all this by experience. Our spiritual state is affected by our physical condition. Man is not spirit only, he is body also. As one of the old Puritans put it, "If you rumple the jerkin, you rumple the jerkin's lining." The penalty for an exhausted body is often a depressed and discouraged soul.

It was so in Elijah's case. Physically wearied as he was, the difficulties of his work appeared more than he could bear, and so he fell an easy prey to spiritual depression. From all of which we may learn a simple, practical, but most salutary lesson. The care of the body—the righteous use of the body—is a religious duty. The observance of the laws of physical health is a Christian obligation. When you sin against the body, either by neglect or indulgence, you sin against the soul. For the body is not a tomb, it is a temple of the Holy Spirit.

Loneliness

But while Elijah's depression was in part due to his physical weariness, it was in far larger measure due to his sense of *loneliness*. There he was in the wilderness, absolutely and utterly alone. And not only physically alone but also spiritually alone for he imagined that out of all Israel he only remained true and faithful to Jehovah. Elijah had felt lifted up and elated on Carmel. For after the fire had come down from heaven and consumed his sacrifice, he had heard the people make their confession—"The LORD, he is the God; the LORD, he is the God" (1 Kings 18:39). For the moment he had been a popular hero, and it was easy to be a prophet of the Lord when all the people were on his side. But the favor of the people had been a fickle and short-lived thing. When Jezebel, the wicked queen, determined to take his life, there was not one out of all the multitude who had applauded him on Carmel to take his part. But Jezebel was able to hunt him as a partridge upon the mountains. And the loneliness of it all nearly overwhelmed Elijah's heart, and he cast himself down beneath the juniper tree and prayed the Lord to take away his life.

Loneliness always tends to *discouragement* and *depression*. "It is not good that the man should be alone" (Gen. 2:18), said the Lord God. And that is more than the justification of marriage. It is the justification of Christian fellowship. "It is not good that the man should be alone." The life of Christian service and discipleship is hard enough at all times. But it becomes ten times harder if you try to live it alone. There is not a young fellow who does not know how terribly hard it is to be true to Christ in the office or the shop when he himself is the only Christian in it. But the whole aspect of things is altered when there is another Christian in the same place of business to sympathize with him and to strengthen his hands in God. Disappointments, difficulties, opposition, mockery—they are not half so hard to bear when we have a friend near to cheer us.

But loneliness is weakening, depressing, heartbreaking. I do not say that there are not men who can pursue their solitary way without flinching or fainting. There have been those who have found all the world against them, as Athanasius did, and who yet have never faltered in their appointed task.

Nevertheless, it remains true that we are all—even the strongest of us—the better for sympathy and encouragement and the touch of kindly hands. Loneliness chills and depresses and weakens. One of the few hints of discouragement that we get in St. Paul's letters we find in his second letter to Timothy, where he writes, "Demas hath forsaken me, having loved this present world. . . . Only Luke is with me" (4:10–11). The loneliness of it all chilled Paul's soul.

And is it irreverent to say that our Lord dreaded loneliness and craved for the encouragement of human companionship and sympathy? What is the meaning of His conduct in the garden but this? Why did He take Peter and James and John along with Him into the recesses of the garden if it was not that He wanted the cheer of their presence? What does that gentle reproach mean with which He chided His sleeping disciples, "Could ye not watch with me one hour?" (Matt. 26:40). I say, what does that mean, save that the Lord craved sympathy, and the way was all the harder for Him because He was left to tread it alone?

Loneliness always tends to discouragement and depression. There are two defenses against it. This is the first—to *remember God*. "Ye . . . shall leave me alone" (John 16:32a), said Jesus to His disciples, and it came literally true, for in the garden all forsook Him and fled. "And yet," He added, "I am not alone, because the Father is with me" (v. 32c). In the strength of God, He trod the sorrowful way to its bitter end, and by the grace of God, He tasted death for every man. "At my first defence," writes St. Paul, "no one took my part, but all forsook me" (2 Tim. 4:16 ASV). And yet, left alone as he was, Paul did not give way to panic or fear. Men left him, but, he adds, "the Lord stood by me, and strengthened me" (v. 17 ASV). That is the most effective remedy for the depression that is born of loneliness—to remember God. After all, we are not alone if He is with us, and we cannot fail if He is with us. We shall be holden up, for He is able to make us stand.

And the second remedy for the depression and discouragement that are born of loneliness is to cultivate *the fellowship of other Christian brothers and sisters.* The Christian life is a social life. It needs fellowship for its vigor and health. I notice that when our Lord sent out His first apostles to preach, He sent them out two and two. Singly they would have been discouraged and would have lost heart because of the difficulties of the service. But in fellowship they found the encouragement they needed. They went forth two and two, and each strengthened the other's hands in God.

I notice in John Bunyan's allegory that he does not make the pilgrims travel to the Celestial City alone. They have company on the way. Christian has Faithful for his companion on the first stage of the journey and Hopeful for his companion in the later stages, while Christiana and her children make the journey in the midst of a great caravan of pilgrims. That is only John Bunyan's way of setting forth the advantages of fellowship. "Iron sharpeneth iron; so a man sharpeneth the countenance of his friend" (Prov. 27:17). Why, I wonder sometimes whether Christian would ever have gotten out of the dungeon of Giant Despair alive had it not been for Hopeful. I also wonder whether he would have crossed the river in safety had it not been for that same helpful friend. It was Hopeful who kept his head above water. It was Hopeful who cheered him with that word, "Be of good cheer, Jesus Christ maketh thee whole," which at last enabled Christian to take courage and win his way to the other side.

The cure for depression is fellowship. It is not good that a man should be alone. And I pass on to you the old advice: "Not forsaking the assembling of ourselves together" (Heb. 10:25). Cultivate the fellowship. It is not a good sign that we are reducing the number of times we gather ourselves together with the people of God. Once-a-week Christians are not, as a rule, the most hopeful and cheerful and robust. Cultivate the fellowship.

It is a tonic for low spirits. I know that again and again when I have been a little discouraged and depressed, to meet at the Lord's Table with my fellow Christians, to gaze into their faces, to realize that they are all living the same life, pledged to the same Lord, engaged in the same service—the realization that I am not alone but one of a great host—has knit thews and sinews of strength in my soul.

Failure

And yet another cause of Elijah's depression was his *sense of failure*. Elijah had one great object in life and that was the winning of Israel back from the vile worship of Baal to the worship of the one true God. It looked at Carmel as if his work was to be crowned with success. But any emotions created there were as fleeting as the early cloud or the morning dew. As soon as the excitement was over, Israel fell back into the old ways. All of Elijah's work seemed to have gone for nothing. Utter and irretrievable failure seemed to dog his steps. He felt as though he had accomplished nothing. All of his labors had been in vain. And the sense of his failure almost broke his heart. "It is enough," he cried. "LORD, take away my life."

And failure, or apparent failure, is still a frequent cause of despondency and depression. We start with great ambitions and vast plans, but we find the world is too strong and stubborn for us. Gradually, the realization that we have failed comes home to us, and with the realization of the failure comes depression and despondency. You remember, perhaps, how the poet describes the disenchanted king:

> He walked with dreams and darkness, and he found
> A doom that ever poised itself to fall,
> An ever-moaning battle in the mist,
> Death in all life and lying in all love.

And the reason for our depression is the apparent failure of our manifold efforts. Our churches have for successive years reported decreases in membership. They are staggering and sobering statistics. And they only reveal a state of things of which many of us were quite conscious even before they were published. And that is what they seem to spell—failure. And many, in face of them, are sadly and sorely discouraged, and are almost tempted to give up the work. Now, I do not want to minimize the significance of statistics like these, and I do not want to encourage a delusive and unwarranted cheerfulness.

But there are two things I would have us ever bear in mind in these dark and troublesome days. This is the first: if it is failure, it is high failure. And high failure is infinitely better than low success. The work is worth the doing if we see no results of it. "I am sure I shall like his way of fighting and being beaten," writes Burne-Jones of a politician still happily left to us; "he would not discourage me a bit—what discourages is a shabby victory." And we may take that encouragement to our hearts—fighting even a losing fight in certain causes is better than winning a shabby victory in others.

And the second thing is this: after all, the failure is only apparent. Elijah discovered, to his amazement, that there were seven thousand in Israel who had not bowed the knee to Baal. And so, too, our Lord's work may be making progress of which we do not dream. Church statistics do not tell the whole tale of the progress of our Lord's kingdom. I do not, of course, minimize their importance. But I repeat that they do not tell the whole tale. Christ has followers of whom the churches take no account. His influence is spreading in ways that cannot be tabulated or expressed in denominational yearbooks. By all means, let us examine ourselves to see wherein we have fallen short of our duty. By all means, let us humble ourselves for our neglects and failures. But let us beware of supposing that the cause is lost or that Christ has failed. Momentary setbacks and reactions there may be, but Christ cannot fail.

It may be, indeed, that the years which record such grave and startling loss, if we knew everything, would prove to be years of great gain. For in various directions I can see the influence of

Christ spreading. In various directions I can see signs of a turning to the Lord. In the growing belief of scientists in the reality of the spiritual, in the evidence we see on all hands of the hunger of the soul for the Infinite, in the ever-growing homage to Christ and the appeal to Him as Master of Conduct and Lord of Society, I see signs of promise and hope. Take the wider view, and you will gain courage, for Christ has not failed.

> Say not, the struggle nought availeth,
>   The labour and the wounds are vain,
> The enemy faints not nor faileth,
>   And as things have been, things remain.
> If hopes are dupes, fears may be liars;
>   It may be, in yon smoke concealed,
> Your comrades chase e'en now the fliers,
>   And, but for you, possess the field.
> For while the tired waves, vainly breaking,
>   Seem here no painful inch to gain,
> Far back, through creeks and inlets making
>   Comes silent, flooding in, the main.